MUSTARD

A TREASURE
FROM BURGUNDY

MUSTARD

A TREASURE
FROM BURGUNDY

FOREWORD
LOUISE PETITRENAUD

TEXT
BÉNÉDICTE BORTOLI

PHOTOGRAPHY
MATTHIEU CELLARD

ABRAMS / NEW YORK

FOREWORD

What would be the only thing I would take with me if I knew I was going to be stuck on a desert island? A pot of smooth Burgundy mustard, of course!

Because I owe everything to that famous little pot: my sensory awareness, my first culinary thrills and my first insights into taste, real taste …

It all goes back to my early childhood. A mouth eating, a face with eyes too big for its stomach. That was me, Loulou, the girl with an unquenchable thirst for flavor – bitter, sweet, acid or salty, I tasted everything.

Then came the day my father handed me that famous spoonful of mustard. The excitement was indescribable. My eyes screwed up, my tongue caught fire, even my cheeks seemed about to ignite as the sensation lingered in my mouth. Then I shivered, blushed, smiled … It was love at first taste.

From then on, mustard and I were inseparable. Every meal would find me reaching into the cupboard for Burgundy mustard. In the kitchen, at table or preparing snacks, mustard was my go-to ingredient.

Then I got angry. To relegate mustard to the condiment category – nothing more than a seasoning – is at best just plain wrong and at worst downright philistine. Mustard is the sliver of gold that makes every taste sublime. It is to food what the gilded decorations of the Hall of Mirrors are to Versailles. Imagine what sausage in brioche would be like without that exquisite soupçon of mustard!

So I thank the Maison Fallot with all my heart – because without their famous little pot of mustard I would not be sharing this love story with you today. But for Fallot mustard, this quintessentially French expertise would not exist and my childhood would simply not have tasted the same.

Louise Petitrenaud

CONTENTS

FROM SEED TO CONDIMENT

AN AGE-OLD TRADITION

A SPICY HISTORY

Mustard seeds, originally known as sénevé (or *sinapi*), were crunched, crushed and mixed with other ingredients before ever they were sold as the potted mustards we know today. They have come a long way since then. The earliest known evidence of their use as a foodstuff dates back at least 5000 years and comes from Central and Western Asia, where various varieties were cultivated as much for their seeds as for their leaves.

Archeological evidence suggests that black mustard seeds first reached Europe (via Germany) in the Neolithic and Bronze Age period (3000-1000 BC). Shortly before 2000 BC they turn up in Egypt, where their status grew from earthly food to celestial food: mustard seeds were placed in the pharaohs' tombs to accompany the newly deceased souls into the afterlife. By the 5th century BC the Greeks were using ground mustard seed as an everyday spice. Mustard greens are also believed to have been ground, then left to macerate in vinegar. As the Romans conquered Europe, they brought mustard seeds along with them, and by the 1st century AD mustard had spread to all parts of mainland Europe. Burgundy, where the Romans also planted vines, is no exception. Archeological excavations continue to provide evidence for the cultivation and widespread use of black mustard seeds in Roman Gaul, of the family *Brassicaceae* (the variety used in our condiment, see pages 42 and 44).

Mustard siliqua.

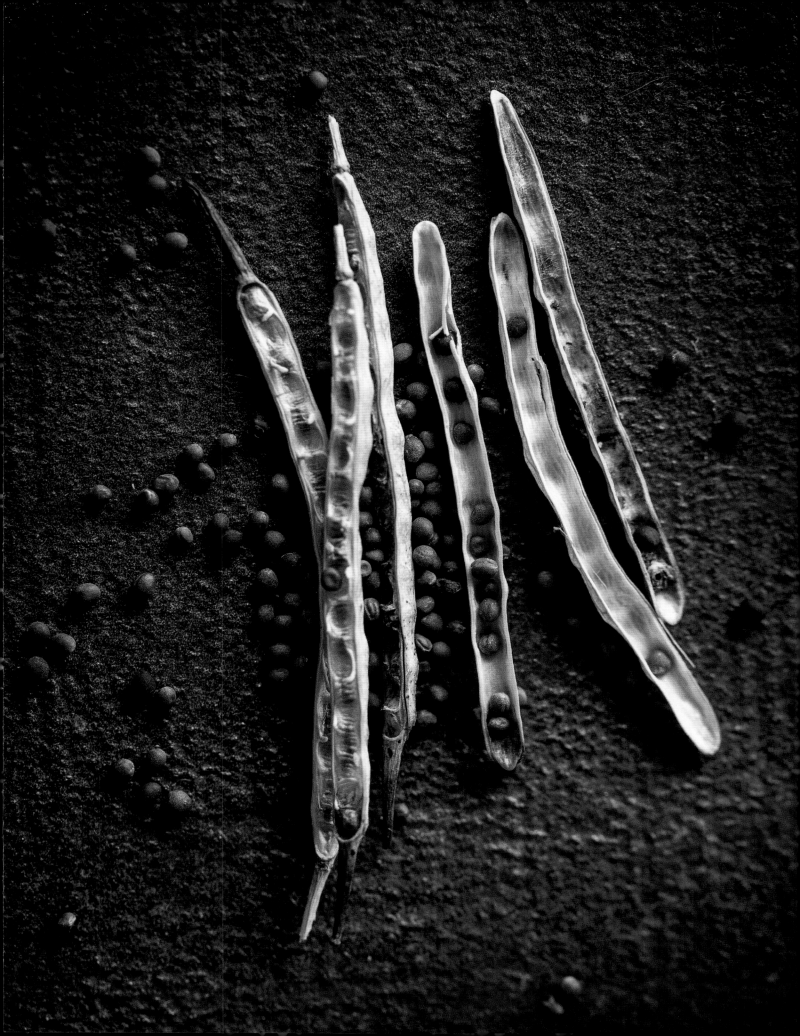

Let's eat!

The first centuries of our era saw mustard seeds used increasingly in recipes (until then, they had been reserved mainly for medicinal preparations). Columella in his Latin treatise on Agriculture *De Re Rustica* (First Century AD) reveals the secrets of "pickling turnips" in a juice based on mustard seeds, and also gives his recipe for a "table condiment" made from ground mustard seeds seasoned with vinegar and mixed with fresh pine nuts and starch. Four centuries later, in the 5th century AD, his fellow Roman Palladius added a little honey and "Spanish oil" to the mix – a recipe that has since become the standard. It seems likely therefore that mustard has been an everyday ingredient since Antiquity, used as a condiment and also as a natural food preservative. We may suppose that ground mustard seeds, mixed with a trickle of vinegar, were used to spice up dishes and preserve pre-cut garden vegetables – just

FOR OUR MEAT-EATING FOREBEARS, SPICY MUSTARD SEEDS WERE A VALUABLE ADDITION TO A WHOLE PANOPLY OF SPICES.

as we now add white mustard to bring out the flavor of sauerkraut, and pickle minicucumbers in mustard sauce. The preparation techniques appear to have been perfected in the Middle Ages, with the monks in particular adding their own tricks of the trade. The use of *verjus* (see page 22) also became common practice. Henceforth, mustard was regarded as a "superior" condiment and sold in towns. For our meateating forebears, spicy mustard seeds were a valuable addition to the panoply of spices, herbs and other seasonings used at the time.

Lie de Vin

Si Vous Voulé de la Moutarde, Ien fais

Verjus

bon Vinaigre

Moulin à Moutarde

Moutarde

boête à la Moutarde

Habit de Vinaigrié,

A Paris, Chez la Veuue N. de L'Armessin, rüe St. Jacq/ à la Pôme d'Or,   Auec priuil du Roy

Vinegar-maker's fancy dress costume featuring the tools of his trade.
Copper engraving attributed to Nicolas de Larmessin (17th Century).

Fiery or victorious origins?

It was not until 1223 that the word "mustard" (from the Latin *mustum ardens*, meaning "burning must") entered the common lexicon as a term for these little seeds in their powdered form: a flour-like substance made from crushed then finely ground mustard seeds that were mixed with grape must to create a paste not unlike the mustard we enjoy today. By the 13th century the term *sénevé* referred solely to whole mustard seeds and so it remained until the 15th century when it was superseded by the term "mustard", referring to seeds and condiment alike. The term *sénevé* is now employed exclusively in biblical and religious contexts.

There is another rather more fanciful explanation for the word "mustard" (though historians have largely dismissed it). It goes like this: in 1383, Charles VI, King of France, called upon Philip the Bold, Duke of Burgundy, to help rescue the besieged court of Flanders. Philip the Bold responded by raising a thousand-strong army of Dijon locals, which he funded through a special tax levied on the then prosperous producers of *sénevé*. After lifting the siege, the Duke of Burgundy commissioned an inscription to be embroidered on his standard, partly to commemorate his victory but also as a reward for the valiant townsfolk. It read: "Moult me tarde", which according to the sources means "I long to return" or "Many await me" (Dijon being the place of return in either case). But due to the standard flapping in the wind, the only legible words when his troops entered the town were "Moult tarde" – or so the story goes. The Duke of Burgundy is also said to have granted local *sénevé* producers the right to display the inscription, together with his coat of arms, on pots of Dijon mustard. The town's flagship product had just been handed its first promotional tool!

The professional *moûtardier* (mustard maker)

In the 13th century, Étienne Boileau, provost of the merchants of Paris, granted Parisian vinegar makers the right to make mustard. Previously, the condiment was exclusively manufactured in Dijon based on the recipe and methods described by Palladius in the 5th century AD. The Dukes of Burgundy were particular aficionados of mustard, which was consumed in such enormous quantities at their banquets in honor of visiting royalty (up to 300 liters/80 gallons at one sitting) that it takes up a whole section of the Ducal Household ledger. It was not long before mustard became popular throughout France and beyond. By the Middle Ages mustard was established in the household kitchen, as evidenced by the many home mustard-seed grinders listed in inventories of inherited family kitchen appliances. Mustard seeds were being ground into flour with pestle and mortar long before coffee grinders found their way into kitchens. The paste could be made at home from scratch, or bought ready mixed but expensively priced from village grocery stores selling mustard paste made from stone-ground seeds, typically using a granite millstone. There were the street vendors too, eagerly peddling their condiments and "bitter preserves" to passers-by.

26

Moutarde.

Itinerant mustard merchant.
Print by Michel Hennin (17th century)

THE POOR MAN'S SPICE AT THE ROYAL TABLE

The lowly mustard seed was never a premium commodity, never got caught up in the shady dealings of the spice race. But it still found its way onto the tables of emperors, popes and all the crowned heads of Europe and France – just as that "least of all seeds" in the Bible grows into the greatest among all herbs.

HISTORY IS FULL OF STORIES ABOUT GRAND FEASTS, complete with detailed breakdowns of the expenses incurred by their powerful hosts. But it does not say much about "ordinary fare". Mustard certainly ranked as a "poor man's" spice in the repertory of medieval food. It was cheaper than salt – then a serious political and economic issue – and all of its more exotic counterparts. While grains of paradise and nutmeg were exclusively reserved for the nobility, mustard made inroads into more modest households that used it to spice up dishes and preserve perishable foods. Clearly therefore, mustard consumption was by no means a marker of status.

Over time, mustard was promoted from accompaniment and ubiquitous dollop on the side of the plate to become the king of condiments that it is today. It is now the most commonly used condiment in the world and the third biggest seasoning after salt and pepper – and the success story continues.

Though long associated with traditional family fare, mustard nonetheless kept pace with culinary trends. Flavored with noble ingredients such as truffles, ceps, Champagne, smooth textured or grainy, strong or mild, mustard has stimulated the creativity of the greatest chefs and tantalized the taste buds of the world's most discerning palates.

Mustard picking.
Italian School (14th century).

It was now the goal to transform a so-called "functional food" – essentially used for its antiseptic properties and as an aid to meat digestion – into an everyday foodstuff. So it was that from the 14th century onward mustard grew ever tastier, not least thanks to the ready availability of vinegar. There followed an array of statutes and regulations ostensibly aimed at protecting public health, but more probably driven by the more venal interests of big manufacturers who feared for their livelihood. In short, mustard-making was no longer open to all-comers.

A number of texts (essentially municipal edicts) dating from this period show that in Dijon, home of mustard, and Orléans, land of vinegar, there was a concerted campaign at local government level to organize the profession and regulate the sale of mustard products. Apothecaries and vinegar makers were grouped into a single corporation (guild), eventually joined by mustard-makers, sauce-makers, spirit distillers and also stall-holders. Members were required to be "sound of limb and neatly appareled", and to conduct themselves in a manner worthy of the

BY THE 16TH CENTURY, MUSTARD HAD BECOME A STAPLE CONDIMENT THAT EVERYONE WANTED.

high-quality ingredients (seeds, verjuice) and utensils that were used in the making of mustard. The statutes also stipulated that mustard must be made of "goodly seeds, soaked in competent vinegar; and when the vinegar used for the soaking thereof shall have lain outside, [the seeds] shall be milled and given a final soak in goodly vinegar, and [the mustard] shall not be sold until the twelfth day following its making." And woe betide anyone who tried to cheat and produce fake mustard ... As evidenced by police reports and fines, professional mustard-makers were kept under very close surveillance.

By the 16th century, mustard had become a staple condiment that everyone wanted. "Without mustard, beef is as tasteless as pike or fried eggs," opines Jean Bruyérin-Champier in 1560 in his cookbook *De Re Cibaria*.

It was around this time that competition from the trade in spices (especially vanilla and nutmeg) led to statutes governing Burgundy vinegar and mustard-makers. Paris meanwhile set an example for others to follow when it recognized mustard making as a profession in 1412. But it was not until 1634, more than 200 years later, that the town of Dijon passed a set of "statutes and orders relating to the activity of the [Dijon] vinegar and mustard maker." Orders, regulations and fines were already in place to prevent fraud. Now these new statutes would put every aspect of their work under very close scrutiny, from equipment and raw ingredients to the skills required of the apprentices and *compagnons* (guild members). The guild entry fees payable by each new apprentice and apprentice master also afforded the town a not inconsiderable source of revenue. The statutes were revised in 1711 to include a string of reforms and obligations, sparking competition between Parisian and Burgundy mustard-makers to introduce new recipes and ever more original flavorings.

In 1756 mustard boomed anew, most notably in Dijon where local mustard-maker Jean Naigeon "made it official" to substitute *verjus* for vinegar – mustard-making back then being rooted in wine country. Naigeon's use of *verjus* fairly revolutionized the flavor of mustard and prolonged its shelf life into the bargain. Small workshops sprang up everywhere in the 18th century, at a time when mustard and vinegar makers were not yet ranked as master craftsmen. By the 19th century, according to the Agenda des Métiers (trade register), most of the workshops were located north of the Bordeaux-Lyon axis. Marseille was the exception, being one of three ports, together with Bordeaux and Nantes, which handled the tuns of mustard exported from France.

BUT IT WAS NOT UNTIL 1634, MORE THAN 200 YEARS LATER, THAT THE TOWN OF DIJON PASSED A SET OF "STATUTES AND ORDERS RELATING TO THE ACTIVITY OF THE [DIJON] VINEGAR AND MUSTARD MAKER."

In 1765 we read in the *Encyclopédie* that Dijon mustard "is considered the best and is widely traded in France." It was then that other towns like Soissons, Meaux, Narbonne and Toulouse started to develop their own production techniques.

Mustard fields at the time were mainly located in Picardy, Flanders, the Paris area, Burgundy, Franche-Comté and Alsace. The Burgundy region was exclusively planted to black mustard and the Bordeaux region to white mustard. Growers elsewhere usually mixed varieties.

In 1853 Maurice Grey invented a machine that speeded up production by automating the laborious sifting of seeds required in the making of Dijon mustard. The production of fine-textured mustard was now possible. Some eighty years later, it was Raymond Sachot who transformed mustard-making from craft industry to mass-production industry. Between them, our benevolent businessmen gave their age-old condiment a new lease of life. Henceforth, mustard was featured at Universal Exhibitions and regional trade fairs alike. Mustard had become a staple of the pantry and consumption has been growing ever since.

VERJUS – PRIDE OF BURGUNDY

Burgundy *verjus*, (verjuice), so called since the end of the 13th century, was the making of locally made Burgundy mustard. In the Middle Ages *verjus* was a basic sauce ingredient.

THE NAME *VERJUS* COMES from the French words for green (*vert*) and juice (*jus*) and denotes the juice of green grapes with an acidic bite – what *Le Littré* 19th century dictionary of the French language describes as "an acidic juice made from unripe grapes and used as a seasoning." For many years *verjus* was extracted from a local grape variety called Bourdelas that gave the juice a very characteristic flavor. Bourdelas was already known in ancient times. Pliny called it the "foolish grape" and Columella's "Bumesta" was probably Bourdelas. In those days, Bourdelas was mainly grown around Dijon, in the Loire Valley and also in the Languedoc. It was mixed with other vines also used to make *verjus*, all of them characterized by large grape clusters and an acidic, rather sour flavor. In Burgundy another *verjus* grape was Le Petit *Verjus*: a member of the Folloides family used to produce Entre-Deux-Mers, and mainly planted for its abundant growth. *Verjus* grapes were also used to make grapes in eau-de-vie, crystallized and glacé grapes, oven- and sun-dried grapes and even jams. In Picardy and Normandy *verjus* was made from the juice of green, unripe apples. In either case, whether based on green apples or grapes, *verjus* owed its acidic bite to the malic acid in the unripe fruit. It was made in barrels by the monastic orders and court attendants, and available to the public from master vinegar and mustard makers. The latter, ever able communicators, made sure to write au *verjus* (made with *verjus*) on their pots of mustard – preferably a locally sourced *verjus*, or better still for the ultimate condiment experience, Clos de Vougeot *verjus*!

The arrival of phylloxera in the late 1800s wiped out Burgundy's Bourdelas plantings, and with them the production of *verjus*. Nobody these days uses green grapes to make *verjus* but the name stuck and now denotes a mixture of vinegar/and or white wine and water.

Vine botanical plate from *Traité Général de Viticulture* by P. and V. Vermorel. Illustration by J. Troncy.

J. Troncy

Verjus

FETISHES, PHARMACY AND MAGIC

Unlike pepper and other much sought-after spices, the humble mustard seed was never traded as money. This was a plant firmly rooted in its French homeland, with none of the exotic connotations of those little berries from mysterious, far-away lands. Mustard was never courted and never bartered – but that that didn't stop it from becoming the most virtuous of them all.

According to popular magic, mustard seeds protected houses, warded off evil spirits and could even exorcise demons. Around 2000 BC, mustard seeds were found in the Egyptian sarcophagi, most probably placed there to protect the deceased and bring them luck. Their market value might be low, but mustard seeds ranked among the most precious of all offerings.

A medicinal plant

The ancients attributed a great many medicinal properties to mustard seeds. They were said to aid the digestion, stimulate the appetite, act as a diuretic, relieve tooth-ache and stomach ache, prevent epileptic seizures and much more besides. Pythagoras ranked mustard among the plants that improve memory, arouse feelings of joy and treat reptile bites. Hippocrates also strongly recommended mustard. Aristophanes ground the seeds into his stews, Theophrastus grew mustard in his kitchen garden and Pliny sang the praises of mustard's many health benefits. With rare exceptions, pretty much everyone agreed with them.

Formation of siliqua and seeds
before the summer harvest.

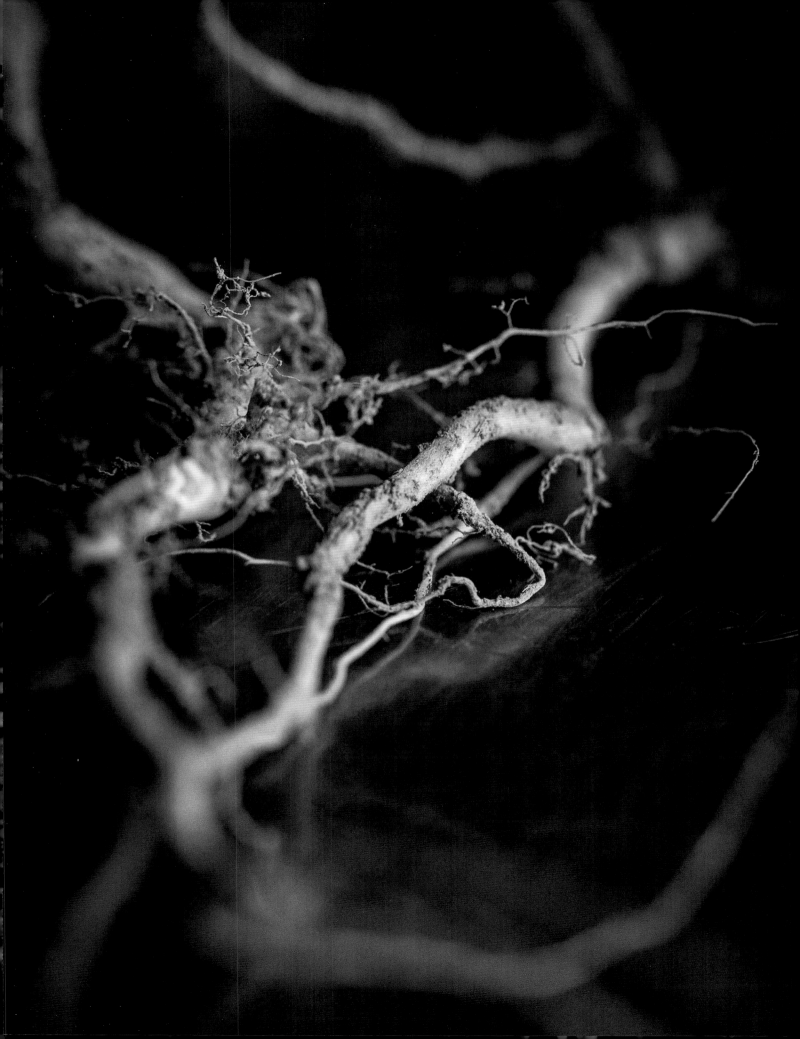

Preceding pages: Mustard greens and roots.

Right: Mustard poultices were available from dispensaries from the 17th century onward and it was a French pharmacist, Paul Jean Rigollot, who invented the mustard plaster (sinapism) in 1866. Known as "papier Rigollot", it consisted of a sheet of strong paper coated on one side with defatted black mustard powder glued down with adhesive. His invention was displayed at the 1900 Paris Exposition, and went on to become hugely popular as a treatment for respiratory disease at a time when tuberculosis ran rampant and the tuberculosis vaccine had yet to be invented (1924).

Setting aside some of the more fanciful claims, it is certainly true that mustard contains essential amino acids, calcium, potassium, vitamins A, B1, B2, PP and trace elements including manganese, nickel, zinc, copper and iron. It is also high in vitamin C (100 mg/100 g) making it a good antiscorbutic.

Records show that in the first millennium (1st to 10th centuries) mustard seeds and mustard greens were required for the making of no less than 292 medicinal compounds.

In the 9th century, Charlemagne (who ate mustard every day) requested that the seeds of this little crucifer that so favored the digestion be sown in the garden of every monastery in Europe, so that he might encounter it wherever he went. Mustard – appetite stimulant, aid to digestion and seasoning all rolled into one – was the best friend of sorely tried stomachs. Since it was believed to be capable of dissolving fats, it also became the basis for every medieval sauce. Rabelais thus depicts a Gargantua (1534) who, with due moderation, has "cast into his mouth […] mustard by the shovelful" after consuming "some dozens of gammons, dried neat's tongues, hard roes of mullet […] andouilles or sausages, and other such forerunners of wine."

Black mustard seeds were ground into flour and used to make poultices. The flour would be sold pressed into bars or loose for mixing to a paste with water, wine or some other liquid, and was hardly ever eaten in France. In English-speaking and Scandinavian countries on the other hand, so-called "dry" mustard was much preferred to the paste version, likewise in hot countries where the paste spoiled easily. Such remedies boomed in the 19th and 20th centuries. Readers of Balzac will remember that in Ursule Mirouët (1842) the doctor tells Madame Bougival to "prepare poultices of ground mustard and apply them to Monsieur's feet."

Flaxseed and mustard poultices were available from dispensaries, which obtained the bulk of their flour from seed merchants and millers. Poultices were widely used to alleviate rheumatism, and general aches and pains. Also, to ease chest congestion by encouraging blood flow to the area of the skin in contact with the diseased organ. Poultices are now rarely used and seem rather old-fashioned. These days it is mainly vets who use mustard powder.

Green manure

Mustard, being a natural soil protector, is ideal as green manure. These are plants grown to protect and improve the soil in the interval between one crop and the next. Green-manure mustard is usually sown in fall immediately after the harvest and offers an all-natural alternative to synthetic crop treatments. Mustard roots, like garlic roots, possess bactericidal and pesticide properties that prevent the spread of plant-parasitic nematodes (roundworms).

The roots penetrate the soil, improving soil aeration and friability and helping to stifle weeds. The still green plants enrich the soil with nitrogen and keep it well supplied with nitrates. They also rid the soil of certain pests. Mustard used for green manure is not harvested, but plowed back into the soil prior to seed set.

NOTHING IS WASTED!

Mustard, as vegetable or condiment crop, has always been consumed in one form or another – greens, seeds, oil or flour.

MUSTARD GREENS are one of the few leafy vegetables that are always in season. They have a tasty, peppery bite and when young and tender can be eaten raw, as a salad or herb. They are less pungent when cooked and can be prepared in the same way as spinach. In Africa and certain parts of Asia for instance, they are chopped and blanched and served as an accompaniment to the main dish. Mustard greens are only ever available locally.

Mustard seeds can be used whole to season or spice up a dish. When fried in oil, they pop open and release all of their nutty flavors. According to Pliny the Elder (First Century AD): "the fried seeds can be used as a ragout [...] cooking removing all of their bitterness." (Translator's note: "ragout", from the verb *ragoûter* is used here to mean "perk up, revive the taste".) Mustard seeds are also a time-honored staple of Indian cooking. In Europe, Asia and the USA, mustard is mainly grown for its seeds, which are used to produce brown mustard. Mixed with other varieties, mustard seeds also serve as bird food and are thought to help chickens lay more eggs. Mustard seeds are oil-bearing. When pressed they release an oil that keeps for a long time without going rancid. In eastern countries, mustard oil is used in cooking, for body massage, as a healing agent, a lubricant, a hair oil and other things besides. It is one of the main cooking oils in Bangladesh, India and Pakistan, where it is much appreciated for its spicy taste. In western countries by contrast, scientists warn against cooking with mustard oil due to its high levels of erucic acid.

Mustard paste, the forerunner of the condiment we know today, was heat and moisture sensitive, spoiled easily and did not travel well. Dry mustard powder on the other hand was easier to ship and became much prized in the French colonial period. Mustard flour had already proved its worth as the basis for poultices (see page 28). Now, when mixed with a little water, it was also said to remove lingering odors from glass bottles and jars (rather like baking soda) and even to deter rats (using a mastic-like filler made from flour to seal the offending holes).

Some of the other uses for mustard are rather more anecdotal in nature. For instance, as a fermenting agent in cider production; and to induce lactation in dairy cows by feeding them mustard root-enriched silage. A multi-purpose plant indeed!

Brown gold.
Burgundy mustard seeds.

THE INDUSTRIALIZATION
OF MUSTARD PRODUCTION

Until the early 19th century, mustard was produced in workshops using mill-stones typically made of granite like those used by millers. The new and emerging technologies also borrowed from the cereal industry, in terms of workspace organization and energy use, and the move toward larger millstones with a corresponding increase in output. Sifting, a feature of the "recipe" for Dijon mustard (see page 54) became ever more refined. Daily production tripled and promised to increase even further after steam turbines made their appearance in France. Packaging followed suit, replacing Grand Feu faience (high-fired stoneware pots hand-painted with a limited range of colors painted onto the raw glaze) with mass-produced faience and glass pots. As the Industrial Revolution took hold, factories were set up that spelled the demise of manual production and the birth of mechanization, most notably electrically driven millstones.

But while working methods evolved and mill wheels turned ever faster, the recipes and manufacturing techniques remained the same as those handed down by craftsmen across the centuries. Revolution In the world of mustard making was an entirely relative concept! It was not until the end of World War II that any significant changes were introduced, starting with the shift toward mustard-making as the core business of small-scale manufacturers that typically sold mustard alongside pickles. Small businesses that resisted modernization were doomed to disappear in favor of newcomers that welcomed industrialization.

Salle de Bouchage et d'emballage des flacons.

REVUE INDUSTRIELLE. — Fabrication de la moutarde et des conserves alimentaires, chez MM. Louit frères, à Bordeaux.

Louit Frères Bordeaux manufacturing works,
Le Monde Illustré, 1865.

Above: Diploma awarded by the 1903 Exposition Internationale to Monsieur Bouley, Monsieur Fallot's predecessor, for the quality of his products.

Opposite: Rare poster by Alfred Choubrac (1853–1902) of the Jules Chéret studio, featuring the "mustard pot with spoon" that was created by the Sens-based firm Maison Méras et Jugnet and for which it filed a patent in 1895 – the year this poster was produced.

From the 1820s onwards, there is evidence of a growing fondness for mustard as a condiment, particularly in urban societies. Laborers who worked in town no longer made mustard at home. Henceforth they bought it from groceries, whose demands had to be met by mustard-makers.

This was the period when many new mustard manufacturers set up business. Everything just fell into place. The equipment (millstone) and raw materials (seeds and locally available *verjus*) were inexpensive. The production facilities (just two rooms, one-up, one-down) were easy to set up and took blessedly little space. Best of all, demand was surging! The time was ripe for the establishment of a business that grasped the potential in mustard and already had a presence in the region selling condiments (gherkins, capers, etc). That business was the House of Fallot.

The birth of an artisan mustard-maker from Burgundy

In 1840 Léon Bouley founded an oil mill and mustard factory that quickly built a solid reputation. In 1923 the Bouley family business was acquired by Auguste Jacob who claimed to have invented mustard "made with pure Burgundy *verjus*" (never mind that this had been around since the 18th century). In 1925 he was succeeded by Paul Chateau who spent the next two years extending the mustard product range to include pickles. In those days the business handled the bulk of the region's gherkins and also canned capers and other condiments. For the future, however, the energies of the business would be focused on the production of mustard, raising it to the ranks of those craft-made products that are the pride of France.

In 1928, the business passed into the hands of Edmond Fallot, grandfather of the present CEO Marc Désarménien. And it has gone from strength to strength ever since, while never losing its human scale. Despite the problems created by World War II, Edmond Fallot boosted business performance by preparing his company for growth. He meanwhile taught his son-in-law and eventual successor, Roger Désarménien, then a newcomer to the team, everything he needed to know about mustard-making. So when Edmond died in 1962, Roger was perfectly primed to pick up the baton and steer the business in the right direction. His guiding principles were those espoused by his father-in-law before him: quality built on tradition; the transmission of values; and the perpetuation of craft skills rooted in the land of Burgundy. The "indomitable man from Beaune" resisted the siren calls and seductive appeal of large-scale retailing (prices, methods of production and volumes). He was determined that quality would never play second fiddle to quantity. Moreover, he was not about to stop doing something that had made the House famous in the first place: crushing its mustard seeds very slowly with millstones. That decision may seem obvious in hindsight but it was a stroke of pure genius at the time!

Poster, 1947, by designer Bob.

Here's proof. In the 1840s, Beaune was home to 32 mustard makers out of some 200 across the region. Today there are just four remaining, and the House of Fallot is the only mustard-maker whose work premises have remained unchanged since that time. Present CEO Marc Désarménien heads up the last independent and family-run *moutarderie* in Burgundy; and having grown up in the family business, he knows where its strengths lie. Since 1994 when his father passed him the baton, he has spared no expense to modernize the production facilities, without ever losing sight of what matters most. In 2003, under his direction, the House of Fallot was among the first players in the food industry to open its doors to the public, with the creation of the very first mustard museum. As the heir to a rich legacy, the Moutarderie Fallot is more than ever rooted in its Burgundy homeland – much to the delight of consumers who are devoted to its family-made products. Fallot mustard is now available in 70 countries worldwide, and every year several tens of thousands of people visit the Moutarderie to discover the intriguing history of this much-loved condiment.

Edmond Fallot
boutique-cum-workshop in Beaune.

GROWING MUSTARD SEED

IN BURGUNDY COUNTRY

FIRST A BIT OF BOTANY...

It's worth remembering that mustard is a plant before ever it becomes a condiment: an annual herbaceous plant of the cruciferous family to be precise, like its relatives, cauliflower, broccoli and horseradish. The flowers are yellow, with the classic mustard-family trait of four petals in a cross, making mustard easy to confuse with rape. The siliques (seed capsules) are densely packed with small brown seeds 1mm (0.03 inches) in diameter having a tough, resistant seed coat.

An all-terrain, unfussy little plant

Mustard is a short-duration crop, with a relatively quick turnaround between sowing and harvest. It is a cool weather plant but doesn't need much water to grow. It also has the merit of being drought-resistant, heat tolerant and frost hardy.

Where does mustard do best? In cool, loose, loamy soils; but it also thrives in the limestone soils of Burgundy.

Plenty of spring sunshine increases the number of seeds per silique but too little water will cause the plant to bolt. In fact, mustard germinates very quickly and can reach over one meter tall (three feet). Modest but prosperous, the mustard seed is exactly as described in the Parable of the Mustard Seed (Matthew XIII, 31-32): "smaller than all the seeds. But when it is grown, it is greater than the herbs and becomes a tree, so that the birds of the air come and lodge in its branches." The fact that the mustard tree of Scripture is now believed to be *Salvadora persica* (known in Syria as the khardal tree) is a botanical nicety and in no way detracts from the symbolic connotations of the image.

Mustard nourishes the soil but also exhausts it, so it must be rotated with other crops. For many years indeed, mustard was mainly used to extract some return from areas of land that were otherwise left vacant.

The *Brassica juncea* species is thought to be a natural hybrid of *Brassica rapa* and *Brassica nigra*. It is one of the Earth's many known species of mustard. In Asia this plant species gives rise to a wide variety of leafy vegetables, among them mizuna.

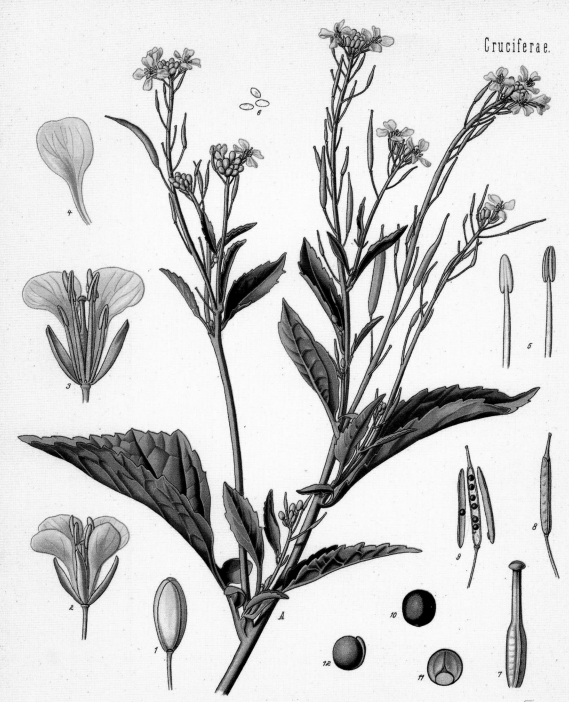

Cruciferae.

Brassica juncea Hook fil. et Thoms.

The seeds used to make mustard condiment

There are some 40 species of mustard, including around a dozen that grow wild across Europe. Of these, the first to be cultivated were two varieties with very different uses: *Sinapis alba*, grown as a green manure and fodder crop; and *Brassica nigra*, used to make the mustard condiment. In World War II it was impossible to import foreign seeds, so French mustard producers used the seeds that grew wild alongside paths. However, a decree was issued in 1937 forbidding the use of white mustard to make the condiment (except in Alsace, in accordance with "local, loyal and constant practice"). So their only option was to use *Brassica juncea*. Brown mustard thus became the principal ingredient in the making of mustard. Higher yielding with a pungent flavor, the fertile *Brassica juncea* offered qualities much prized by mustard mills like the Moutarderie Fallot. Only the seeds serve to make mustard, roughly 1.5mm (0.05 inches) in diameter so scarcely bigger than those of its black counterpart.

Mustard flower, spring.

SELECTING
THE SEEDS USED
TO MAKE MUSTARD CONDIMENT

Research undertaken in the 1990s in Burgundy (see page 55) relating to the selection and genetic improvement of seeds has established the core criteria for scientists, growers and mustard-makers alike. The key factors are as follow:

Good yield per hectare: vital to ensure that mustard-growing remains competitive compared to other crops used in the food industry.

Cold tolerance: essential for varieties sown in fall.

Early-flowering: particularly important to limit pest damage by the Pollen Beetle (*Meligethes aeneus*) and ensure higher yields.

Plant height: short varieties are easier to treat as they grow, easier to harvest and the stems are less likely to break.

Disease resistance: essential to prevent the sometimes devastating yield losses caused by disease.

The Thousand-Seed Weight (TSW): the accepted standard weight for 1000 mustard seeds is 2.3 grams (0.08 ounces). The heavier the seed, the easier it is to sow, harvest and sort. Heavier seeds also produce more paste and make the mustard-maker's job easier.

Sinigrin content (see page 86). Sinigrin is the compound that gives mustard its pungent taste.

Oil content: this must be kept low to avoid spoiling the paste.

Protein content: essential for good paste performance (the lower the protein content, the higher the oil).

Erucic acid concentration: this should be little or nothing, as erucic acid may be a risk factor for cardiovascular disease.

Paste viscosity and dry-extract content (as measured by a desiccator).

Kernel and seed color (aiming to produce a paste that is neither too dark nor too pale).

On the basis of these criteria, new seed varieties are created and tested every year by the agricultural industry in order to select the most stable and high-performance varieties.

MUSTARD,
BURGUNDY'S HERITAGE

Until the middle of the 19th century, French mustard production relied on black or white mustard seeds or a mix of the two. It was not until 1850 that the first seeds arrived from Russia and the former British India and were blended, usually as a pair, with their Western European counterparts. Russian seeds were shipped in sacks and said to be cleaner.

In the late 19th and early 20th century, black mustard (*Brassica nigra*) was cultivated for its seeds in various departments of Northern France, such as the Bas-Rhin, Charente, Picardy and also Bourgogne-Franche-Comté, where it was grown in small fields on the Côte-d'Or – in total less than 800 hectares of plantings, mainly confined to farms on the plateau areas. Until World War Two, Burgundy growers sowed their mustard seeds close to charcoal-burning mounds as the ashes contained potash that helped the plants to grow. But as industrialization ramped up, the charcoal burners gradually disappeared and with them the potash required by the region's small mustard mills. With local mustard farming falling into decline, producers resorted to planting seeds from outside the region (mainly from the Marne, Somme, Seine-et-Oise, Loire and Indre), then from abroad. The preferred source was the Canadian province of Saskatchewan, where the mustard seed was only introduced in the 1940s. But by 1960, seed yields from the Côte d'Or – just six hectares of mustard fields on the plateau areas between Salives and the Arrière-Côte – were no longer enough to maintain local production of mustard as a condiment. Despite burgeoning demand from the mustard industry, Burgundy's mustard fields looked set to disappear altogether. With the domestic supply chain under pressure, producers imported seeds from Holland, Rumania, India (Bombay) and Italy (mainly Bari, in the Apulia region, for mild to semi-strong mustard), these latter two varieties being especially rich in oil. Henceforth, mustards were often made from a blend of seeds of different origins.

EDMOND FALLOT

DEPUIS 1840

GRAINES de MOUTARDE
DE BOURGOGNE

A BEAUNE, BOURGOGNE

FRANCE

Dijon "recipe"

It took several decades for Burgundy producers to organize themselves and mount a robust defense of their mustard's unique character. But for all its worldwide reputation, Dijon mustard has yet to be granted protected denomination status. It is simply a "recipe", as defined by a French decree of 10 December 1937 stipulating a dry-extract content (black or brown seeds, salt and spices) of at least 28% and a seed integument content (seed husk residues) of at least 2%. Its production process is characterized by sifting or winnowing (*tamisage/blutage*): the stage when mustard seeds are separated from the husks, then ground and steeped in vinegar. In July 2000, a new decree introduced even tighter criteria for mustard production. Most notably, it defined four classifications: Moutarde à l'Ancienne, Moutarde Verte, Moutarde Violette and Moutarde Brune.

Dijon mustard does not have protected denomination status (the patent having expired) so can be made anywhere. Just as Savon de Marseille can be produced in Singapore or New York, there is nothing to stop Dijon mustard being made in the USA, Japan or Russia, from seeds of different origin. The Moutarde de Dijon appellation was above all a sales ploy, even if did play a big part in building the town's reputation and remains forever linked with the history of Burgundy.

But we had not heard the last from our little Burgundian seed ...

IN THE LATE 19TH AND EARLY 20TH CENTURY, BLACK MUSTARD (*BRASSICA NIGRA*) WAS GROWN FOR ITS SEEDS IN VARIOUS DEPARTMENTS OF NORTHERN FRANCE, SUCH AS THE BAS-RHIN, CHARENTE, PICARDY AND ALSO BOURGOGNE-FRANCHE-COMTÉ ...

Cock-a-doodle-doo!

The 1940s saw the first attempts to revive mustard farming in the departments of the Loiret, Loir-et-Cher, Cher and Burgundy, using Alsatian, Italian, Russian, Rumanian and Indian seed samples. But with the outbreak of war, the priority was no longer to test plants, even less spices and herbs that were still considered secondary commodities. After the war, a number of Burgundy mustard-makers launched into production of a paste made from a mixture of wild mustard (*Sinapis arvensis*, the variety that grows alongside paths), with white wine or vinegar. At the time, mustard mainly served as a cover crop on fallow land, in rotation with other crops. The last plots of brown Burgundy mustard gradually disappeared from the region in the 1950s. Because mustard farming was not very profitable, it was abandoned in favor of plants that were eligible for EU subsidies, such as rape and wheat.

BY THE 1980S THERE WAS NOT A SINGLE HECTARE OF MUSTARD PLANTINGS LEFT.

By the 1980s there was not a single hectare of mustard plantings left. It would take until 1986 for varietal selection work to get underway, starting with the appointment of a senior lecturer in crop improvement at the then École Nationale d'Ingénieurs des Travaux Agricoles (ENITA), now Agrosup. In taking a botanical inventory, our researcher discovered some fifty packets of brown mustard seeds (Brassica juncea) that carried a precise description of the contents. They turned out to be Burgundy varieties that had been quietly slumbering in their wrappers for decades. This decided the Burgundy Chamber of Commerce to revive the planting of native seeds. A steering committee was formed bringing together all members of the industry; a laboratory of plant genetics was set up at the school; and a team of dedicated individuals was appointed to run the project. The research participants included the Institut National de la Recherche Agronomique (INRA – National Institute of Agricultural Research), with financial support from the Conseil Régional de Bourgogne (regional council of Burgundy). Using the recently discovered seeds, some 200 parental lines were planted on experimental plots within the school. Their performance was then monitored for the purposes of seed characterization and cross-breeding. Based on the data collected, three cultivars were added to the *Catalogue Officiel des Espèces et Variétés* (national catalogue of species and varieties) listing the seeds grown in the period 1993-1995.

Following intensive seed trials in Canada, it was time to reintroduce the local variety. But first, farmers had to be persuaded to try something new – an ambitious, long-term project that called for close collaboration between the handful of scientists, growers and mustard-makers involved.

In the 1990s, 18 farmers got together to make the project happen. The idea of reviving mustard farming in Burgundy also earned the support of the Maison Fallot, ever a torchbearer of the region's heritage and a true ambassador for the native mustard variety. Burgundy's heirloom seed was accordingly sown anew, with plantings increasing from six hectares in 1960 to 30 hectares in 1992, then 1,500 hectares in 2008. The period 1993-1997 then saw little change in the area under mustard (roughly 250 hectares). However since 1998, based on research revealing the importance of fall sowing, the area under mustard like the number of mustard farms has been steadily increasing. The Burgundy project's success also owes much to the development of higher-yielding, more cold-tolerant varieties, supported by EU funding since 2006, and growing demand from a local industry specializing in Burgundy mustard-seed processing.

Today Burgundy is home to 6,000 hectares of mustard-seed plantings and nearly 300 mustard producers. Annual yields exceed 10,000 tonnes and 15 varieties are grown, including three that are now approved for the production of mustard awarded PGI status (Protected Geographical Indication). Five moutardiers meanwhile remain more committed than ever to protecting Burgundy's mustard industry. These are Maison Fallot, Européenne de Condiments, Reine de Dijon, Unilever Bestfood France (Amora-Maille) and Charbonneaux Brabant. The region additionally produces some 90,000 tonnes of so-called "strong" mustard paste from seeds across all categories – that's 90% of domestic production and 50% of EU-wide production.

THE IDEA OF REVIVING MUSTARD FARMING IN BURGUNDY ALSO EARNED THE SUPPORT OF THE MAISON FALLOT, EVER A TORCHBEARER OF THE REGION'S HERITAGE AND A TRUE AMBASSADOR FOR THE NATIVE MUSTARD VARIETY.

Façade of the Moutarderie Fallot – the historic building dating back to 1840 where all Fallot mustard is still produced today. Pictured here with a 1930s Peugeot SK parked outside.

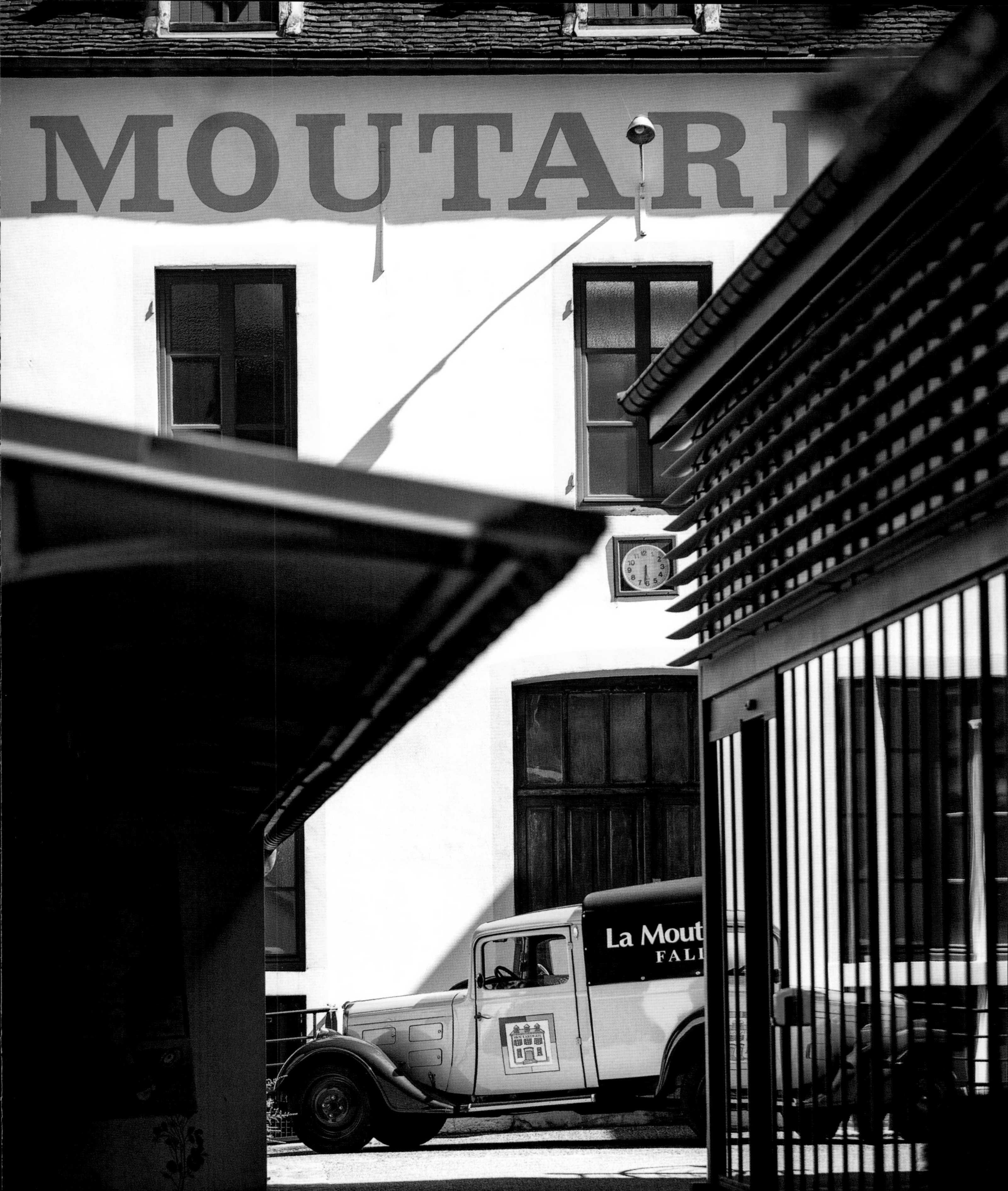
MOUTARI
La Mout
FALL

Mustard of Burgundy PGI

The awarding of Protected Geographical Indication (PGI) in 2009 has placed Burgundy mustard among those local flagship products that are deeply connected to their place of origin – with an exemplary carbon footprint into the bargain!

Unlike Dijon mustard that can be made anywhere in any manner, Burgundy mustard is subject to a strict set of rules. The seeds must be registered in the official French catalogue of species and varieties. Producers must comply with detailed specifications and ensure the traceability of seeds up to the point of delivery, as also must the *organismes stockeurs* (crop storage facilities). Certified seeds must be set aside in special cells. Species selection is determined by plant trials conducted by the industry, together with the testing of mustard paste by manufacturers. As the world grows ever more aware of the disruption caused by climate change, we need to make the right decisions for the planet's sake. Those of us in the mustard industry face many challenges ahead as we strive to enshrine our new approach in Burgundy's farming heritage.

Burgundy mustard is made using dry white wine with Protected Designation of Origin (PDO) from the Burgundy wine region. Wine content must be at least 25% of total fluid content. Such noble ingredients aside, Burgundy mustard may also contain salt, spices and other additives approved for use in food in the EU. The dry extract content of the seeds must equal at least 24% of finished product weight; the seed lipid content must equal at least nine percent of finished product weight; and husk residue must not exceed two percent of total paste weight.

Mustard-seed storage and paste production (processing) must take place in the defined geographical area. The mustard growing area is even more restricted, and confined to the interior of Burgundy.

PGI status has so far only been granted for the smooth, sifted mustard, but producers are now asking the INAO for recognition of old-style, whole-grain mustard made from 100% *graines de Bourgogne* (100% Burgundy seed).

For the consumer, the "Mustard of Burgundy" PGI designation is the only guarantee that the mustard was produced in Burgundy, using Burgundy seed. Merchandizing marks such as "Made in France" in no way guarantee the French provenance of the ingredients – seeds, for instance.

Burgundy mustard, characterized by its light yellow color, thick, smooth creamy texture, strong bite and aromas of white Burgundy wine, is a jewel in the crown of regional culinary heritage.

Opposite: Ceramic jars, earthenware jars, glass jars, tubs – mustard takes great care of its appearance. *Habillage* (the packaging that "dresses" up the product) is a key element of brand identity.

Following pages: left, L. Bouley & Cie mustard pot (1850); right, Fallot mustard pot ready to grace the table (1960).

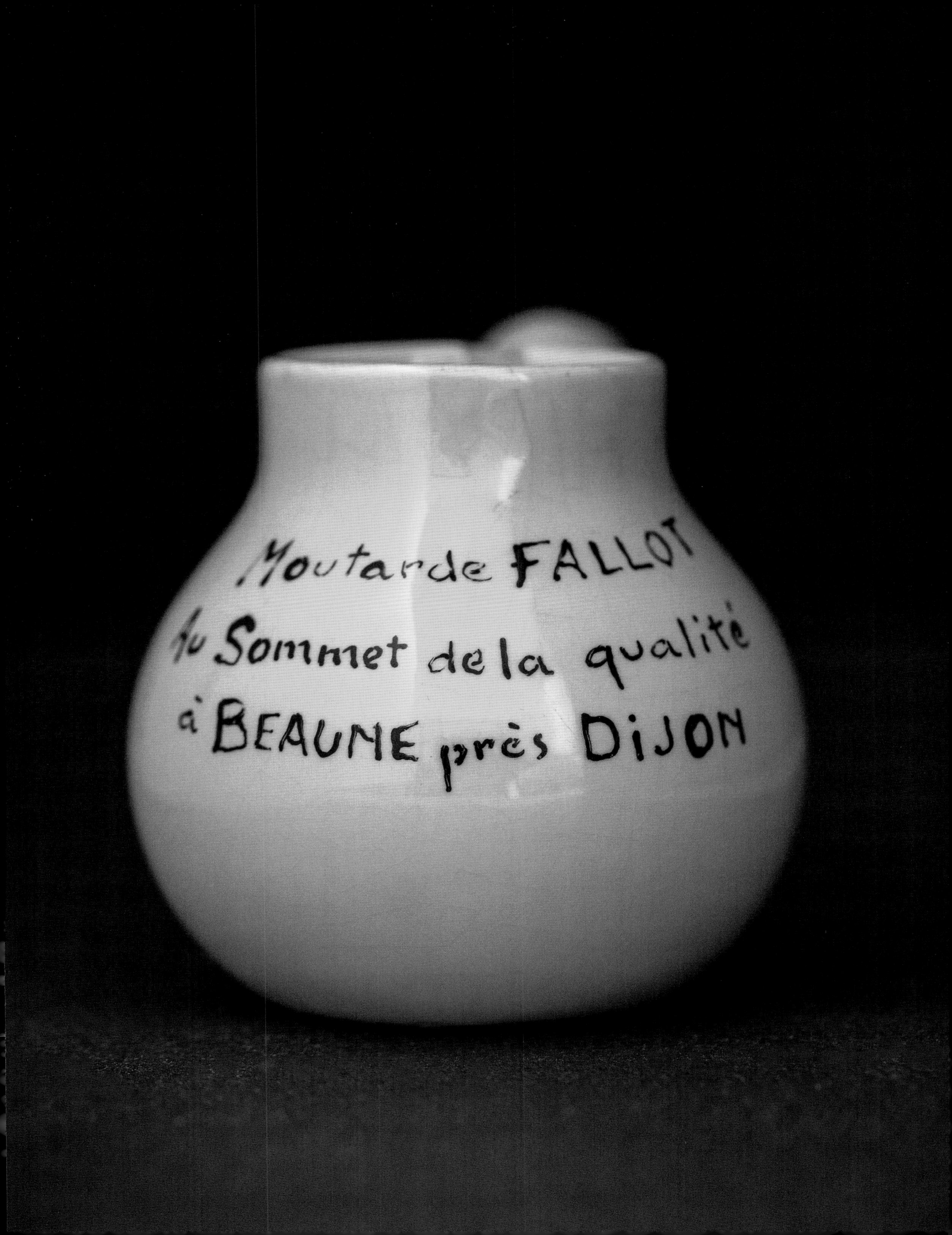
Moutarde FALLOT
Au Sommet de la qualité
à BEAUNE près DIJON

THE MUSTARD LANDSCAPE: HERE AND ELSEWHERE

The land of Burgundy is ideally suited to mustard growing and now accounts for 90% of French mustard production. That's 6000 out of some 6,500 hectares of French mustard plantings, reflecting Burgundy's policy to reintroduce the local seed variety.

BUT BURGUNDY is no longer alone in its efforts. Other regions that are now following suit, albeit on a much smaller scale, are the departments of Seine-et-Marne, Eure-et-Loire and Ardèche, the regions of Vexin and Le Perche and the fields around Orléans, France's vinegar capital.

Canada was for many years the top producer and exporter of mustard seed but recent years have seen a fall in Canadian output. Since 2018 Canada has ranked second to Nepal for mustard seed production. Nepalese production is reserved for the domestic market and finds applications in areas other than the production of mustard condiment – most notably massage oils with so-called analgesic properties, and hair treatments. India is the country with the largest variety of mustard seeds.

In France, eight out of 10 people are regular mustard users (roughly two pounds per person per year) and nearly 20 pots of mustard are sold domestically every minute. But the country where mustard sells best is not France but America – the home of fast food. Fallot mustards are available on all continents, on land and also in the air, courtesy of the airlines that carry the House's family-made condiments. More than 50% of the House's production is exported, with the bulk of it going to the USA. The family's hall of fame includes Germany, a producer and consumer of mild, sweet mustard; and Japan, a major producer of wasabi.

TRADE SECRETS

OLD AND NEW

A DELICIOUSLY SIMPLE RECIPE:
THE TRADITIONAL WAY
TO MAKE MUSTARD

Just three ingredients are required to make mustard: mustard seed (kernel and husk); *verjus* (see page 22), which serves as the binder; and brine, which serves as a flavor enhancer. The basic principles have survived unchanged for centuries, as also has the recipe despite minor variations due to changing fashions, available ingredients and advances in food preservation.

The kernel accounts for 80-85% of seed weight. It contains protein, soluble sugars and fat (remembering that mustard seed is oil-bearing).

One kilogram of seeds (2.20 lbs) is enough to produce three kilos (6.60 lbs) of mustard. Fallot mustards are known for their high seed content and contain a higher proportion of whole seeds – so more kernel, for a naturally stronger bite.

Early twentieth century mustard-making
equipment. Museum area of the Moutarderie Fallot

Millstones are the basis of the Maison Fallot's ancestral manufacturing technique, testament to an artisanal know-how that informs every stage of the production process. Traditional millstone grinding prevents the seeds from overheating, so producing a mustard with a texture and taste like no other.

STAGES IN THE MUSTARD PRODUCTION PROCESS

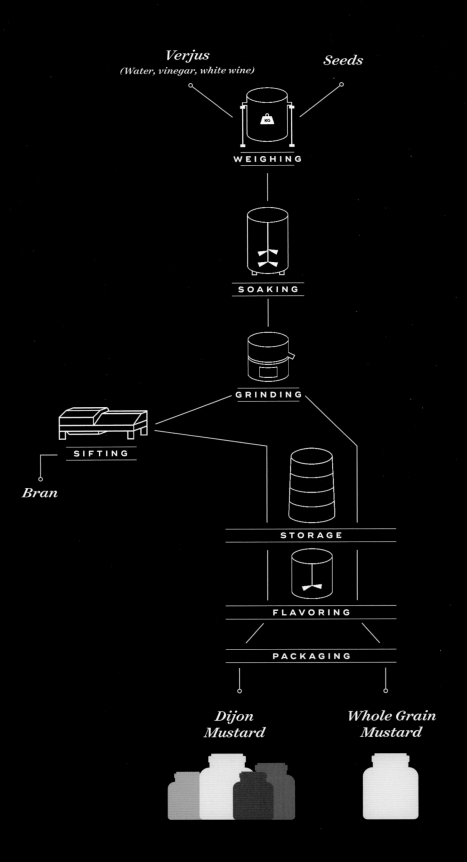

Verjus
(Water, vinegar, white wine)

Seeds

WEIGHING

SOAKING

GRINDING

SIFTING

Bran

STORAGE

FLAVORING

PACKAGING

Dijon Mustard

Whole Grain Mustard

Seed cleaning

After silo storage the seeds are sorted in a winnower to remove any impurities (dust, stones, broken seeds, etc), then graded and cleaned using seed cleaning screens.

Soaking in *verjus*

This stage is optional but executed at the Moutarderie Fallot because it softens the seeds and makes it easier to separate the kernel from the husk.

Grinding

The soaked seeds are ground between a pair of millstones: a revolving upper stone called the "turning runner stone" and a fixed, stationery bottom stone called the "bed-stone". This produces a paste-like substance still containing bran. (Millstones remain widely used by artisanal mustard producers, unlike industrial manufacturers that typically use synthetic grinding wheels.)

Sifting

The paste is squeezed by means of rollers through micro-perforated turbine blades that eliminate the bran. This is the operation that transforms coarse-grain mustard into smooth-textured Dijon-style mustard (coarse grain mustard is also known as "whole grain" or "old style" mustard because the paste still contains the kernel and husk).

Flavoring (optional)

These two types of mustard – old-style grainy and smooth – serve as the basis for a variety of styles, which in turn allow for a range of flavorings (see page 78).

Resting the paste and kneading

The paste is set aside to rest before bottling to reduce the bitterness and bring out the aromas in the mustard. It is then gently kneaded to remove any air bubbles and avoid the risk of oxidation.

Packaging and shipping

The paste is poured into the appropriate container (jar, tub, etc) by an automatic filling machine. Next comes labeling, packaging and shipment. The condiment is now ready for sale, stamped with a "best before" limit of approximately 18 months.

Artisanal mustard producers like the Maison Fallot produce around 500 kilos (1000 lbs) of mustard paste per hour. Some of their industrial counterparts can produce ten or twelve times as much!

FLAVORING
AN AGE-OLD
PROCESS

Mustard makers have been adding flavorings for ages – honey in ancient and medieval times; spices in the Renaissance period; flowers in the 17th century; then nasturtiums, lemon, anchovies – whatever it took to keep pace with the new craze for sophisticated mustards and herb-infused "mixed" vinegars. This continues today. The head of production at an artisanal *moutarderie* is something of a chef on the quiet. The ingredients are added in the order given in the recipe; certain ingredients are still weighed by hand; and the appearance of the mustard (texture, color) and bran are regularly checked and to see if any adjustments are needed. Mustard recipes vary in complexity and call for different quantities of herbs and spices. Mustards flavored with Pinot Noir are among the most difficult, taking great care to add the ingredients in the right order.

From top to bottom and left to right: Cassis Dijon mustard; green tarragon mustard; Madras curry mustard; saffron mustard; Espelette pepper mustard; whole grain mustard with white wine, with honey, with Modena Balsamic Vinegar, with Burgundy Pinot Noir, with *Marc de Bourgogne* and with Dijon gingerbread

100% BURGUNDY

Fallot mustards contain a good number of Burgundy specialties. Added ingredients may include Noir de Bourgogne blackcurrants, Crémant de Bourgogne sparkling wine, gingerbread and truffles – to mention but a few.

Blackcurrants have been growing in the Beaune region since the middle of the 18th century. Noir de Bourgogne is an exceptionally fragrant local blackcurrant variety, which is used to produce liqueurs and perfumes and also as a medicine (the leaves are said to relieve rheumatic pain and gout). The tiny blackcurrant is packed full of vitamin C (200 mg/100 g), calcium, magnesium and potassium. It is also very easy to digest thanks to its high fiber content.

The gingerbread was reputedly introduced to France in the 14th century by Margaret III, Countess of Flanders and wife of Philip the Bold, Duke of Burgundy. Mad about gingerbread, she is believed have traveled to France with her pastry chef in tow so that she could continue to enjoy her *boichet* (as it was known then). Burgundy gingerbread is made with wheat, honey, eggs and sugar but the recipe varies widely depending on region and country.

MUSTARD CRAFTING
BEHIND THE SCENES

Mustard, for all of its associations with traditional cooking, is the focus of considerable research and positively fizzes with creative possibilities. An artisanal family firm like the Maison Fallot brings out a new variety of mustard every year. Driving innovation is Fallot's young CEO Marc Désarménien, who reckons it takes about six months to bring a product to market, sometimes less depending on the year of harvest. Take for instance the House's latest offering, Penja pepper mustard. The idea to create a mustard based on a pepper with Protected Geographical Indication (PGI) was conceived in June. Then came two months of testing in July and August, followed by product release in early December. Testing at the Fallot Moutarderie is initially conducted in the in-house laboratory. The first step is the selection of the mustard base (Dijon mustard, whole grain mustard, etc) or more rarely, the creation of a new mustard. For the pepper mustard, the Production and Quality Control Department opted for Dijon mustard. The next stage was to combine the mustard with the appropriate type of peppercorn. Out of several preselected varieties, four were specifically chosen for their organoleptic properties. Preliminary manual testing was then carried out in the laboratory, focusing on small product samples that were meanwhile tasted by the team, checking the appearance, nose and palate of the different peppers on offer. Pigment-rich peppers that made the paste too dark were eliminated. Likewise peppers with invasive aromas or an overly pungent bite.

Marc Désarménien, grandson of Edmond Fallot and Chief Executive Officer of the Moutarderie Fallot, pictured here with his two sons Yvan and Thibault.

Following a rigorous selection process, a supplier was appointed subject to a strict set of rules, and the information they provided concerning inputs (in this case, pepper) was verified and approved to check compliance with mandatory labeling requirements. The mustard was then "registered" (described in a datasheet listing its organoleptic properties, nutritional value, allergen content, etc) and monitored for quality assurance purposes at every stage of production. Its shelf life was assessed to determine the Best Before Date (BBD, printed on the packaging) and to check color and flavor stability.

Another key stage after product approval is packaging and labeling design: at Fallot, every pot of mustard must look as good as it tastes! This is when all of the ingredients are listed (together with their amounts as a percentage of the total) and the recipe fed into a computer before going into production. Labeled and clearly identifiable, the newly launched mustard will now be monitored on an ongoing basis to make sure performance complies with processing industry standards.

Mustard is ever ready to innovate as tastes in mustard change, the while upholding its tradition of quality. One hundred percent plant-based, mustard is ideally poised to take its place among the foods of tomorrow, turning even the most delicate confection into a truly sublime tasting experience.

Edmond Fallot blackcurrant Dijon mustard.

WHY DOES MUSTARD GO UP YOUR NOSE?

A few basic notions of chemistry suffice to explain this effect of mustard – which recalls the expression of annoyance "gets right up my nose", referring to something that enters the nasal passages and causes pain or irritation.

LET'S START with a bit of chemistry. Mustard owes its pungency to allyl isothiocyanate, an aroma molecule that is formed through the action of grinding the seeds with liquid (*verjus* or a mixture of vinegar, white wine and water – see above). This releases two molecules contained in the seed, myrosinase and sinigrin, triggering a chemical reaction that produces allyl isothiocyanate, which is not otherwise present in the seed. Allyl isothiocyanate is also found in other foods that go up your nostrils and make you cry – wasabi and horseradish and to a lesser extent arugula. When we eat mustard, allyl isothiocyanate travels up into the nasal cavity and stimulates the trigeminal nerve, irritating the nose, eyes and mouth, then titillating the sensory receptors.

To check this out for yourself, take a whiff of a small handful of mustard seeds. You will find that they are completely odorless. But if you crush a few between your teeth, mixing them with your saliva in the process, you will taste a bitterness – quickly followed by bite!

Another thing you should know is that heat is no friend of mustard. Warm temperatures destroy its intrinsic piquancy, which is highly volatile and disappears entirely at 40-50°C (104-122°F). The natural piquancy of mustard is a sign of freshness and good quality but it doesn't last forever no matter how airtight the jar. Hot mustards are indeed a part of French culture, never mind that modern tastes tend more toward the milder versions.

Fallot's unmistakable packaging: the little metal bucket, forerunner of its plastic counterpart, still marketed by the Moutarderie today!

MUSTARD
IN GASTRONOMY

40 CHEF RECIPES

Mustard has a place in every kitchen. No picnic or bistrot table is complete without it. And mustard's credentials are now recognized by the best chefs in the world.

Mustard will bring out the flavor of the most delicate fare, which is a far cry from its more traditional associations with rich charcuterie, gargantuan banquets and rabbit smothered in mustard. Mustard is the basis for a whole range of sauces, goes beautifully with seafood and vegetables and adds a touch of spice to sweet flavors. Flavored mustard plays on matching flavors one minute, contrasting flavors the next. And that's not all, because mustard has many surprises up its sleeve – not least as the spiciness that makes a recipe memorable.

The people whose business it is to titillate the taste buds – those high-flying chefs, cooks, pastry-cooks and barmen, in France and elsewhere – now invite you to discover the savory delights they have created around exceptional mustards.

PHILIPPE AUGÉ
HOSTELLERIE DE LEVERNOIS AND
BISTROT DU BORD DE L'EAU – LEVERNOIS

PATRICK BERTRON
LA CÔTE D'OR – SAULIEU

DANIEL BOULUD
DANIEL – NEW YORK

JEAN-RÉMI CAILLON
KINTESSENCE – COURCHEVEL

JEAN-MICHEL CARRETTE
AUX TERRASSES – TOURNUS

LUCILE DAROSEY
LOISEAU DES DUCS – DIJON

OMAR DHIAB
LOISEAU RIVE GAUCHE – PARIS

RUBÉN ESCUDERO
MANKO – PARIS

WILLIAM FRACHOT
WILLIAM FRACHOT – DIJON

MOURAD HADDOUCHE
LOISEAU DES VIGNES – BEAUNE

COLIN LACH
MONSIEUR MOUTARDE – DIJON

CHRISTOPHE MULLER
PAUL BOCUSE – COLLONGES-AU-MONT-D'OR

AYMERIC PINARD
LA CÔTE D'OR – SAULIEU

ÉRIC PRAS
MAISON LAMELOISE – CHAGNY-EN-BOURGOGNE

**GUILLAUME QUENZA
AND MATTHIEU BIRON**
FRÉQUENCE – PARIS

SYLVAIN SENDRA
FLEUR DE PAVÉ – PARIS

KEISHI SUGIMURA
LE BÉNATON – BEAUNE

MICHEL AND CÉSAR TROISGROS
LE CENTRAL – ROANNE

LOUIS-PHILIPPE VIGILANT
LOISEAU DES DUCS – DIJON

PHILIPPE AUGÉ
HOSTELLERIE DE LEVERNOIS
LEVERNOIS

SCALLOP AND SHELLFISH *BONBONNIÈRE*
WITH CREAMY GINGERBREAD AND HONEY DIJON MUSTARD SAUCE

SERVES 4

FOR THE *BONBONNIÈRES*
4 celery roots
1 carrot, finely chopped
1 onion, finely chopped
1 ½ cups (5 oz./150 g) finely chopped celery
¼ cup (1 ¾ oz./50 g) butter
1 cup (250 ml) white wine
1 cup (250 ml) chicken stock
Salt and freshly ground pepper

FOR THE SHELLFISH MARINIÈRE
1 lb. 2 oz. (500 g) mussels
1 lb. 2 oz. (500 g) cockles
1 lb. 2 oz. (500 g) clams
3 shallots, finely chopped
¼ cup (1 ¾ oz./50 g) butter
A few parsley sprigs
2 cups (500 ml) white wine

FOR THE CREAMY SAUCE
1 cup (250 ml) whipping cream
⅓ cup plus 1 tbsp. (3 ½ oz./100 g) Gingerbread and Honey Dijon Mustard

FOR THE SCALLOPS
12 scallops
1 tbsp. hazelnut oil
4 tsp. (¾ oz./20 g) butter
Salt and freshly ground pepper

FOR THE *BONBONNIÈRES*
Preheat the oven to 360°F (180°C). Slice the tops off the celery roots and set them aside. Hollow out the celery roots. In a casserole dish, sweat the chopped carrot, onion, and celery in the butter, then add the celery roots. Season with salt and pepper. Pour in the white wine and the chicken stock. Bake, covered, for about 12 minutes. Remove from the oven, remove the chopped vegetables and liquid from the casserole and reserve the celery roots.

FOR THE SHELLFISH MARINIÈRE SAUCE
Rinse the mussels, cockles, and clams. In a saucepan, sweat the shallots in the butter. Add the shellfish and the parsley, then pour in the white wine. Cook, covered, for a few minutes, until all the shells have opened. Remove the mussels, cockles, and clams from their shells and reserve the broth.

FOR THE CREAMY SAUCE
In a saucepan, slightly reduce 2 cups (500 ml) of the reserved shellfish broth. Add the cream and let it reduce again. Emulsify the sauce with the mustard. Keep it warm.

FOR THE SCALLOPS
Shuck the scallops and remove the meat. Rinse the scallops under cold running water, then dry with kitchen towel. Heat the hazelnut oil in a skillet. Season the scallops with salt and pepper then, when the oil is hot, place them in the pan. Sear the scallops until golden, then add the butter.

TO SERVE
Reheat the celery roots and the mussels, cockles, and clams. Divide the shellfish between the celery roots, then add the scallops. Emulsify the sauce and pour it over the seafood.

Chef's note
I chose to use Gingerbread and Honey Dijon Mustard because it marries perfectly with the slightly nutty flavor of the scallops.

PHILIPPE AUGÉ
BISTROT DU BORD DE L'EAU
LEVERNOIS

PARSLEY HAM IN ASPIC JELLY
WITH SEED STYLE MUSTARD CREAM

SERVES 10

PARSLEY HAM
(prepare the day before)
4 ½ pounds (2 kg) pork shoulder
4 pig's trotters
2 carrots
2 onions
1 head of garlic
1 lb. 2 oz. (500 g) leeks
1 thyme sprig
1 bouquet garni
1 lb. 2 oz. (500 g) shallots
10 garlic cloves
2 bunches of flat-leaf parsley
Olive oil
¾ cup (7 oz./200 g) seed style mustard
1 ¼ cups (300 ml) sherry vinegar
Salt and freshly ground pepper

FOR THE ASPIC JELLY
2 bunches of flat-leaf parsley

FOR THE MUSTARD CREAM
1 cup (250 ml) whipping cream
½ cup plus 1 ½ tbsp. (5 oz./150 g) seed style mustard

TO SERVE
A few radishes, halved
5 oz. (150 g) baby frisée leaves
Olive oil
Slices of *pain de campagne* (French sourdough)

FOR THE PARSLEY HAM

The day before, blanch the pork shoulder and the pig's trotters in two separate pans. Preheat the oven to 280°F (140°C). Peel and finely chop the carrots, onions, and garlic. Finely chop the leeks. Place the shoulder and the pig's trotters in a casserole dish and add the chopped vegetables, thyme sprig, and bouquet garni. Pour in enough water to cover and cook in the oven for 4 hours.
Check the meat for doneness: it should be very tender. Remove the meat from the casserole dish, then strain the gravy through a fine-mesh sieve and set aside. Remove the meat from the pig's trotters and dice the shoulder.
Peel and finely chop the shallots. Peel and chop the garlic. Chop the parsley leaves and stalks. In a saucepan, brown the shallots and garlic in a drizzle of olive oil. Leave to cool. Blend half of the trotter meat, then add it to the pan. Finally, stir in the mustard, vinegar, and parsley. Season with salt and pepper.

TO ASSEMBLE THE TERRINE

Cut the remaining trotter meat into small pieces. In a terrine dish, layer the diced shoulder, chopped trotter meat, and the meat-and-parsley mixture. Place a weight on top of the terrine and refrigerate overnight.

FOR THE ASPIC JELLY

The next day, heat 6 ½ cups (1.5 liters) of the reserved cooking juice in a saucepan. Chop the parsley and add it to the pan. Leave to cool slightly.
Remove the terrine from the refrigerator, unmold it, and pour over a third of the warm parsley jelly. Refrigerate the terrine. Repeat this step three times. The terrine should have a nice shine.

FOR THE MUSTARD CREAM

Whip the cream, then stir in the mustard. Refrigerate until ready to serve.

TO SERVE

Place a slice of terrine on each plate, then add some radish halves and a few frisée leaves seasoned with a drizzle of olive oil. Serve with a quenelle of mustard cream and a slice of toasted *pain de campagne*.

Chef's note
The potency of the seed style mustard goes perfectly with the pork flavors.

PATRICK BERTRON
LA CÔTE D'OR
SAULIEU

CHUCK STEAK
WITH CEP MUSHROOM AND BLACK TEA MUSTARD

SERVES 6

FOR THE BEEF

2 ½ lb. (1.2 kg) chuck steak

2 ¾ oz. (75 g) carrots

2 ¾ oz. (75 g) onion

1 garlic clove

Scant ¼ cup (50 ml) duck fat

4 tsp. (20 g) butter

2 tbsp. all-purpose (plain) flour

2 cups (500 ml) red wine

1 bouquet garni

2 tbsp. cep mushroom and black tea mustard

Salt and freshly ground pepper

FOR THE VEGETABLES

6 carrots

7 tbsp. (3 ½ oz., 100 g) butter

Scant ½ cup (100 ml) chicken bouillon

30 small button mushrooms

Scant ¼ cup (50 ml) white wine

1 red onion

Scant ½ cup (100 ml) red wine

4 tsp. (20 ml) wine vinegar

10 ½ oz. (300 g) chanterelle mushrooms

Salt and freshly ground pepper

FOR THE BEEF

Preheat the oven to 360°F (180°C). Tie the chuck steak into a roll and season it. Peel the carrots and onions, then dice them. Peel the garlic.

In a casserole dish, brown the beef in the duck fat on all sides for 5 minutes, then remove it. Add the butter to the casserole dish with the carrot and onion and sweat gently for 5 minutes. Season. Sprinkle with the flour and brown lightly, stirring all the time. Pour in the red wine and a little water and bring to a boil. Return the chuck steak to the casserole dish: it should be half immersed in the cooking juices. Add the bouquet garni and garlic.

Cover and bake in the oven for 3 hours, checking that the liquid remains at the same level. Remove the chuck steak from the casserole dish and allow it to cool for 3 hours.

Strain the cooking juices through a fine seive, pour them into a frying pan, and stir in the mustard. Bring to a boil and check the seasoning.

FOR THE VEGETABLES

Peel the carrots, then cut them into small cones or thin sections. Sweat them for 2 minutes with a little butter in a frying pan. Add the chicken bouillon, season, and cook, covered. Check they're done by pricking them with the tip of a knife: they should be tender.

Remove the stems from the button mushrooms and peel the caps. Sweat the mushroom caps in the butter, deglaze with the white wine, and season. Cook for 10 minutes.

Peel the red onion and cut it into strips. In a saucepan, heat the red wine and vinegar until boiling. Remove from the heat, add the onion strips, and leave to marinate for 1 hour.

Wash the chanterelle mushrooms in plenty of water and drain them. Just before you're ready to serve, sauté them in the remaining butter.

TO SERVE

Cut the chuck steak into six slices, then heat it up in the mustard sauce, without boiling it. Reheat the vegetables and serve them with the steak on hot plates.

Chef's note

Cep mushroom and black tea mustard adds an autumnal touch to this classic Burgundy recipe.

VEAL CHOP WITH BABY CARROTS
AND CILANTRO AND CANDIED ORANGE MUSTARD JUS

SERVES 4

FOR THE CILANTRO AND CANDIED ORANGE MUSTARD JUS

1 scant cup (200 ml) veal bouillon

2 tbsp. cilantro and candied orange mustard

1 tbsp. carrot purée

4 cilantro leaves

1 tsp. grated orange zest

Salt and freshly ground pepper

FOR THE CARROTS

4 baby carrots

1 ¾ tbsp. (1 oz./25 g) butter

⅝ cup (150 ml) chicken bouillon

4 coriander seeds

1 garlic clove, peeled

Salt and freshly ground pepper

FOR THE VEAL CHOPS

2 ¾ tbsp. (40 ml) duck fat

2 milk-fed veal chops (14 oz./400 g each)

2 tbsp. (30 g) butter

Salt and freshly ground pepper

TO SERVE

8 baby Swiss chard leaves

FOR THE CILANTRO AND CANDIED ORANGE MUSTARD JUS

Slightly reduce the veal bouillon to intensify the flavor. Add the mustard, then thicken the jus by stirring in the carrot purée. Cook for 4 to 5 minutes. Stir in the chopped cilantro leaves and the grated orange zest. Season with salt and pepper.

FOR THE CARROTS

Peel the carrots, leaving ¾ inch (2 cm) of the tops intact. Using a melon baller, scoop out the center of each carrot to ¼ inch (5 mm) deep along its entire length. Blanch the carrots for 2 minutes in a saucepan of boiling salted water.
In a sauté pan, heat the butter, then turn the carrots in it for 2 minutes. Pour in the chicken bouillon and add the coriander seeds and the garlic clove. Season with salt and pepper. Leave to cook gently, then check the doneness using the tip of a knife.

FOR THE VEAL CHOPS

Preheat the oven to 360°F (180°C). In a large casserole dish, heat the duck fat. Salt and pepper the veal chops, then brown them for 5 minutes on each side. Add the butter. Finish cooking in the oven for 3 to 4 minutes on each side. Remove the veal chops and let the meat rest for 10 minutes at room temperature.

TO SERVE

Just before serving, reheat the veal chops in the oven in the casserole dish for 3 to 4 minutes, then remove and slice them. Arrange the carrots on the plates and cover them with a few baby Swiss chard leaves. Pour a little mustard jus onto each plate and carefully arrange the veal on top.

Chef's note
The cilantro and candied orange mustard goes remarkably well with veal and carrots—the perfect match!

PATRICK BERTRON
LA CÔTE D'OR
SAULIEU

CILANTRO AND CANDIED ORANGE
MUSTARD CREAM

SERVES 4

FOR THE MUSTARD CREAM

1 scant cup (200 ml) whipping cream

A little cilantro and candied orange mustard

Salt and freshly ground pepper

TO SERVE

1 Little Gem lettuce

1 tub of fresh herbs

3 tbsp. walnut oil vinaigrette

4 slices of *paté en croûte*

FOR THE MUSTARD CREAM

Whip the cream using a hand or electric whisk. When it is firm, stir in the mustard to taste. Season with salt and pepper. Spoon the mustard cream into a pastry bag fitted with a medium tip, then refrigerate for 1 hour.

TO SERVE

Cut the Little Gem in quarters. Separate the leaves, wash them under running water, then drain. Wash the herbs, add to the lettuce leaves, and season the salad with the walnut oil vinaigrette.

Arrange the salad on the plates. Cut each slice of *pâté en croûte* in half and arrange them, overlapping, on the plate. Using the pastry bag, pipe dots of mustard cream around the edge of each plate.

Chef's note

This flavored-mustard cream adds freshness and subtlety to *pâté en croûte* and other charcuterie.

CHAUD-FROID OF FREE-RANGE POULARDE

WITH ARTICHOKE BARIGOULE, TARRAGON DIJON MUSTARD, LENTIL SALAD, AND BATAK BERRIES

SERVES 8

FOR THE POULARDE
(prepare the day before)
2 ¼ lb. (1 kg) poularde breast, skin removed
1 tbsp. (½ oz./14 g) salt
1 scant tsp. (2 g) ground pepper

FOR THE CONSOMMÉ
2 small white onions, halved
2 ½ lb. (1.2 kg) chicken meat, preferably legs, cut into large pieces
2 small leeks, white part only, diced
2 carrots, diced
1 bunch of parsley
2 thyme sprigs
1 bay leaf
2 ½ tsp. salt
14 egg whites
8 ½ pints (4 liters) chicken stock
2 cloves
10 coriander seeds
8 cracked black peppercorns
2 garlic cloves, crushed
2 tbsp. dry sherry vinegar
Salt and freshly ground white pepper

TO ASSEMBLE THE TERRINES
2 cups and 3 tbsp. (520 ml) of consommé
7 sheets of gelatin

FOR THE POULARDE

The day before, prepare a *bain-marie* at 144°F (62°C). Season the poularde with salt and pepper on all sides, then transfer it to a sous-vide bag. Vacuum seal the bag and submerge it in the *bain-marie*. Leave to cook for 1 hour. Let the chicken cool at room temperature for 15 minutes, then immediately refrigerate it. When it is completely cool, remove the chicken from the sous-vide bag and cut it into ¼ inch (5 mm) thick slices. Refrigerate.

FOR THE CONSOMMÉ

In a cast-iron pan over high heat, place the onion halves cut-side down and cook until blackened, about 4 minutes. In a food processor, combine the blackened onions, chicken meat, leek, carrot, parsley, thyme, bay leaf, and salt. Add the egg whites and continue to mix until you obtain a paste. Pour this mixture into a 7-quart heavy-bottomed cooking pot and whisk in the chicken stock, cloves, coriander seeds, cracked black peppercorns, and crushed garlic. Cook over medium heat, scraping the bottom of the pot regularly with a rubber spatula to prevent the meat from sticking. Once the liquid reaches a light simmer, cook, undisturbed, until the mixture begins to form a solid mass or "raft" on the surface. Gently poke a hole in the middle, large enough to pass a small ladle through it. Allow the consommé to simmer gently for 30 minutes, occasionally ladling it over the raft using the hole in the middle. To strain, carefully ladle the consommé through a fine-meshed sieve lined with three layers of damp cheesecloth set over a clean pot. Stir in the sherry vinegar, salt, and pepper.

TO ASSEMBLE THE TERRINES

Bring 2 cups and 3 tablespoons (520 ml) of consommé to a boil (refrigerate the remainder to use for the *chaud-froid*). Soak the gelatin sheets in iced water for about 5 minutes. Once the gelatin sheets have bloomed, melt them into the hot consommé and turn off the heat. Let the liquid cool to room temperature then immerse the poularde.
To assemble the terrines, you will need a silicone éclair mold about 16 x 12 inches (40 x 30 cm) with 14 inserts of 5 x 1 inch (12 x 2.5 cm). Place the mold on a baking sheet and begin layering the sliced poularde inside all the way up to the top.
You will need three or four layers, depending on the thickness of the slices. Cover the terrine with the cooled consommé and refrigerate overnight.

DANIEL BOULUD
DANIEL
NEW YORK

FOR THE *CHAUD-FROID*

3 cups and 3 tbsp. (750 ml) consommé

1 cup (250 ml) whipping cream

¼ cup (2 ¼ oz./60 g) butter

½ cup (2 ¼ oz./60 g) all-purpose flour

15 sheets of gelatin

A few Batak berries

Salt and freshly ground pepper

FOR THE ARTICHOKES

Scant ½ cup (100 ml) olive oil

1 onion, diced

8 garlic cloves

2 ¼ lb. (1 kg) small artichokes, cleaned

1 bunch of tarragon

1 scant cup (200 ml) white wine

2 cups (500 ml) water (or chicken stock)

2 lemons

2 tbsp. salt

1 scant tsp. ground pepper

FOR THE ORANGE GARNISH

1 orange

Juice of 2 oranges

5 tsp. (¾ oz./20 g) superfine sugar

4 tsp. (20 ml) Sauternes wine

Salt

FOR THE CRISPY LENTILS

⅔ cup (4 ½ oz./125 g) dry lentils

Salt

FOR THE *CHAUD-FROID*

The next day, mix the 3 cups and 3 tablespoons (750 ml) of consommé with the cream, then bring to a boil. Make a roux: melt the butter in a saucepan over low heat and, when it begins to sizzle, pour in the sifted flour all at once. Crumble this roux into the boiling liquid and whisk briskly until the mixture thickens. Remove the pan from the heat and season with salt and pepper. Soak the gelatin sheets in iced water then stir into the mixture. Leave this liquid at room temperature until you are ready to glaze. Remove the terrines from their silicone mold and place them on a wire rack placed on a baking sheet. When the *chaud-froid* is at room temperature, glaze the terrines several times until they are evenly coated. On the last glaze, sprinkle the ground batak berries over each terrine then refrigerate.

FOR THE ARTICHOKES

Pour half the olive oil into a large saucepan and sauté the onion and garlic over low heat until translucent. Add the artichokes and tarragon, deglaze with the white wine, and reduce the liquid by half. Add the water (or chicken stock) and the lemon juice. Season with salt and pepper, bring to a boil, and simmer until the artichokes are tender.

Remove the artichokes from the hot liquid but reserve this for later use in the lentil puree. Slice the artichokes in half and dry them well. Sear them in a skillet in the remaining olive oil. Season with salt and pepper then refrigerate.

FOR THE ORANGE GARNISH

Using a peeler, gently peel the orange to remove the outer zest, being careful to leave behind the white pith underneath. Blanch the zest three times in boiling water, then combine the zest, juice, sugar, and wine in a pot. Bring to a boil, cook for 4 minutes, then remove from the heat. Strain the orange zest and cut part of it into 16 diamond shapes of ¾ inch (2 cm). Place the remaining zest into a blender and puree until smooth with a small amount of liquid. Season with salt and place in a pastry bag until ready to use.

FOR THE CRISPY LENTILS

Preheat the oven to 122°F (50°C). Combine the lentils with the water and bring to a boil, then simmer for 12 minutes. Drain the lentils, place them on a baking sheet and dry in the oven for at least 2 hours. Then fry the dehydrated lentils in a deep fryer at 347°F (175°C) and drain well. Season with salt.

FOR THE LENTIL SALAD AND PUREE

2 ⅔ cups (1 lb. 2 oz./500 g) dry lentils

4 ¼ cups (1 liter) water

2 ½ tbsp. (1 ½ oz./40 g) tarragon Dijon mustard

1 ¾ oz. (50 g) celery, cooked and diced

1 ¾ oz. (50 g) carrots, cooked and diced

A few drops of Pedro Ximénez sherry vinegar to taste

Salt and freshly ground pepper

FOR THE TARRAGON MAYONNAISE

2 oz. (55 g) egg white (about 2 medium egg whites)

Scant ½ cup (110 ml) tarragon oil

Scant ½ cup (100 ml) grapeseed oil

1 tbsp. olive oil

A few drops of Tabasco and lemon juice

Salt and freshly ground pepper

TO FINISH

Tarragon Dijon mustard

A few tarragon leaves

FOR THE LENTIL SALAD AND PUREE

In a saucepan, combine the lentils with the water and bring to a boil, then simmer for 15 minutes. Season with salt, then add the mustard, celery, and carrots. Continue cooking for an additional 5 minutes, then season with pepper and the sherry vinegar.
Place half the cooked lentils in a blender, adding just enough strained water from the artichokes to create a smooth puree.

FOR THE TARRAGON MAYONNAISE

Combine the egg whites in a blender and slowly stream in the tarragon oil, grapeseed oil, and olive oil until a thick mayonnaise is formed. Season to taste with the Tabasco, lemon juice, salt, and pepper and store in a pastry bag until ready to use.

TO SERVE

When ready to serve, cut the terrines into 1 ½ inches (4 cm) slices, then place two slices on each plate. Garnish each slice with a piece of candied orange zest and a few crispy lentils.
Place three small mounds of the lentil salad on the plate.
Then top each lentil salad with a piece of seared artichoke and place two small quenelles of tarragon mayonnaise on opposite sides of the plate.
Decorate with alternating dabs of tarragon mustard, lentil puree and orange confit puree, then place a small leaf of tarragon alongside the mustard dabs and serve.

Chef's note

Mustard plays a vital role in many French recipes. It is such a unique ingredient that we rely on it to give depth to many recipes. This Tarragon mustard is even more special. It's a sharp, aromatic, tangy, vibrant, complex, refined, savory ingredient that I always have available at home. Adding Tarragon mustard to a salad dressing or a sauce transforms a home-cooked dish into something deliciously unique at the drop of a hat!

SPRUCE-SMOKED LAVARET (WHITEFISH)
WITH SMOTHERED LEEKS AND EXTRA-STRONG BEAUNE MUSTARD *GRENOBLOISE*

SERVES 4

FOR THE LAVARET
2 ¼ lb. (1 kg) scaled and gutted lavaret

1 tbsp. (5 g) juniper berries

2 cups (1 lb. 2 oz./500 g) coarse salt

9 oz. (250 g) fresh spruce sprigs plus
a little sawdust

Scant 1 cup (7 oz./200 g) clarified butter

¾ oz. (20 g) extra-strong Beaune mustard

Salt and freshly ground black pepper

FOR THE SMOTHERED LEEKS
2 ¼ lb. (1 kg) leeks

⅓ cup (2 ¾ oz./75 g) clarified butter

1 tbsp. (15 g) salt

FOR THE *GRENOBLOISE*
2 ¾ oz. (75 g) lemons

¾ oz. (20 g) mustard greens

3 tbsp. (¾ oz./20 g) nonpareil capers

2 ¼ oz. (60 g) white bread croutons

FOR THE MUSTARD COULIS
¾ oz. (20 g) mustard greens

2 tsp. water

1 tsp. extra-strong Beaune mustard

½ tsp. white vinegar

Salt and freshly ground pepper

FOR THE LAVARET
Lift the lavaret fillets and remove any small bones. Mix the juniper berries and coarse salt, then sprinkle a little of this mixture into a dish. Place the lavaret fillets in the dish and cover with the remaining salt and juniper berry mixture. Refrigerate the fillets for 20 minutes, then rinse under cold running water.

Place a little sawdust in a smoker and top with the spruce sprigs. Place the lavaret fillets on a rack and smoke them for 25 minutes. If you don't have a smoker, place the sawdust and spruce sprigs in a dish or casserole dish, light with a blowtorch, lay a rack on top and place the fish fillets onto it. Cover the dish with plastic wrap, or the casserole dish with its lid, and monitor the cooking process. In a dish, heat the clarified butter to 129°F (54°C). Dip the lavaret fillets in the butter then poach them for 6 to 7 minutes (they should be slightly pink). Keep them warm.

FOR THE SMOTHERED LEEKS
Preheat the oven to 360°F (180°C). Wash the leeks, then discard the green leaves using only the tender white parts. Wrap the leeks in parchment paper with the clarified butter and salt, then wrap again in foil. Bake in the oven for 25 minutes. Leave to cool for 1 hour at room temperature. Cut the leeks into even lengths and split them lengthwise.

FOR THE *GRENOBLOISE*
Finely dice the lemon flesh and reserve the juice. Finely chop the mustard greens. Stir all the ingredients together to make a *grenobloise*.

FOR THE MUSTARD COULIS
Blend all the ingredients together, then strain through a fine sieve to obtain a smooth coulis. Season with salt and pepper.

TO SERVE
Season the lavaret fillets with sea salt and freshly ground pepper. Drizzle a line of mustard on each plate, then arrange the lavaret fillets on top.

Drain the leeks and arrange them on the plates. Add some *grenobloise*. Add some mustard coulis next to the lavaret.

Chef's note

According to Savoy tradition, river fish belonged to the owner of the waterways - abbey, lord or bishop. At that time, noble fish—lavaret, fera, and trout—were the preserve of the great houses.

In this recipe, inspired by traditional French cuisine, the delicacy of the lavaret flesh cooked à la *grenobloise* is subtly spiced by the mustard and enhanced by home-grown winter leeks.

PRALOGNAN SOUP

WITH MUSTARD GREENS AND SEED STYLE DIJON MUSTARD

SERVES 4

FOR THE PEA SOUP
(prepare the day before)

1 cup (7 oz./200 g) *pois blonds*
(French dried peas)

1 ¾ oz. (50 g) onion (about ⅓ cup chopped)

1 ¾ oz. (50 g) celery (about ½ cup chopped)

1 ¾ oz. (50 g) carrot (about ⅓ cup chopped)

¼ cup (1 ¾ oz./50 g) butter, diced

1 ¾ oz. (50 g) bacon, chopped

Salt and freshly ground pepper

FOR THE MUSTARD CREAM

Scant ½ cup (100 ml) heavy cream

2 ½ tbsp. (1 ½ oz./40 g) mascarpone

2 ½ tbsp. (1 ½ oz./40 g) seed style Dijon mustard

Scant ¼ tsp. (1 g) wasabi paste

1 tsp. (5 g) grated horseradish

Salt and freshly ground pepper

TO SERVE

Mustard greens

FOR THE PEA SOUP

The day before, soak the dried peas in cold water overnight. The following day, peel and roughly chop the onion, celery, and carrot. In a saucepan, melt the butter, then add the chopped vegetables and bacon. Cover the pan and lightly brown over low heat. Drain the peas, place in a pan, and cover with cold water. Bring to a boil and cook over low heat until the peas are just tender. Remove from the heat and allow to cool for 1 hour at room temperature.

Drain the peas, reserving the cooking broth. Set aside about ⅓ cup (2 ¼ oz./60 g) of the cooked peas. Blend the remaining peas with some of the cooking broth until you obtain a smooth soup. Strain through a fine sieve. Season to taste with salt and pepper.

FOR THE MUSTARD CREAM

Whip the cream using a hand mixer. Fold in the mascarpone with a spatula, then stir in the mustard, wasabi, and horseradish. Season to taste with salt and pepper.

TO SERVE

Divide the reserved cooked peas among four soup plates, then pour over the soup.

Using a tablespoon, form a quenelle of mustard cream and place it in a small bowl. Top with a few mustard greens.

Serve the soup with the mustard cream, which will season it and enhance its flavors.

Chef's note

At one time, whole fields of peas were grown in the Savoy valleys. In wintertime, people would often make soup from these *pois blonds*, to which they would add bacon or a ham bone. This Dijon mustard seemed to me to be an obvious addition to this country-cooking-inspired recipe.

JEAN-MICHEL CARRETTE
AUX TERRASSES
TOURNUS

CRISPY CREPE
WITH DIJON MUSTARD BUTTER AND ORGANIC RADISH

MAKES 12

CREPES
2 eggs
2 tsp. (10 g) butter
¾ cup (100 g/3 ½ oz) all-purpose flour
Pinch of salt
1 cup (250 ml) milk
2 tsp. water

FOR THE MUSTARD BUTTER
¼ cup (1 ¾ oz./50 g) butter at room temperature
4 tsp. (¾ oz./20 g) Dijon mustard
Salt and freshly ground pepper

TO SERVE
1 organic black radish
1 tbsp. yellow and black mustard seeds
A few mustard sprouts

FOR THE CREPES
Mix all the ingredients together in a mixing bowl, then let the batter rest for 2 hours in the refrigerator.
Heat a panini press and pour a little batter onto the plate, being careful that it doesn't flow over the edges. Cook for about 3 minutes. If the crepes are not crispy enough, dry them in the oven at 140°F (60°C) for about an hour. Cut them into rectangles about 6 inches long by 1 ½ inches wide (15 x 4 cm).

FOR THE MUSTARD BUTTER
In a mixing bowl, using a spatula, beat the butter until soft and creamy. Stir in the mustard and season with salt and pepper. Transfer to a pastry bag.

TO SERVE
Wash the radish, remove any rootlets and tops, then finely chop. Using the pastry bag, pipe lines of mustard butter into the folds of the crepes and sprinkle with the chopped radish. Garnish with a few mustard seeds and sprouts.

Chef's note
Coming from Burgundy, for me it was an obvious choice to use a mustard butter—from Dijon, of course— to create an appetizer full of pep.

JEAN-MICHEL CARRETTE
AUX TERRASSES
TOURNUS

FARM-RAISED RABBIT FILLET
RUBBED WITH TARRAGON DIJON MUSTARD

SERVES 4

1 farm-raised rabbit saddle
(about 1 lb. 2 oz./500 g)

Grapeseed oil

1 thyme sprig

1 shallot

2 pink garlic heads

½ cup (120 ml) dry white wine

4 ¼ cups (1 liter) chicken or rabbit stock

1 tbsp. Dijon mustard

2 knobs of butter

½ bunch of chervil

½ bunch of dill

½ bunch of cilantro

¼ bunch of mint

7 oz. (200 g) fresh spinach leaves

¼ cup (2 ½ oz./70 g) tarragon Dijon mustard

3 ½ oz. (100 g) pork caul fat

2 small red onions, peeled

Olive oil

Salt and freshly grated nutmeg

Preheat the oven to 320°F (160°C).

Remove the fillets from the rabbit saddle and trim them. Crush the carcass and cut the trimmings into small pieces, then brown them in a saucepan with a drizzle of grapeseed oil. Once the pieces are well browned, add the thyme, the shallot cut in quarters, and one head of garlic cut in half. Deglaze with the white wine, using a wooden spoon to scrape up the browned residues from the bottom of the pan. Pour in the stock to cover the meat and leave to reduce over a low heat. Strain the gravy through a fine sieve, then return to the pan and continue to reduce. Stir in the Dijon mustard and 1 knob of butter. Keep this gravy warm.

Trim, wash, and dry the herbs, then chop them coarsely.

Wash and trim the spinach leaves.

Brush the rabbit fillets with the mustard, roll them in the mixed chopped herbs, then wrap them in the caul fat.

Place the remaining head of garlic and the onions on a baking sheet and roast them in the oven for 30 minutes to caramelize. Remove the tray from the oven, then separate the garlic cloves and cut the onions in half and separate the petals.

Just before serving, brown the rabbit fillets in a sauté pan with a drizzle of olive oil. Finish cooking them in the oven for a few minutes, checking to ensure that the meat remains juicy. In the same pan, lightly sauté the spinach with a knob of butter. Prick a garlic clove on a fork and stir the spinach with it. Season with salt and a pinch of grated nutmeg.

TO SERVE

Cut each rabbit fillet into six rounds. Arrange some spinach and two pieces of rabbit on each plate, then add a few caramelized onion petals and garlic cloves. Serve the gravy in a gravy boat.

Chef's note

I wanted to reinterpret my father's rabbit with mustard recipe using tarragon Dijon mustard, which adds both a spicy and a delicate note. You can also place a dab of tarragon mustard on the edge of each plate.

MADRAS CURRY MUSTARD-GLAZED SQUASH SLICE
WITH SHELLFISH

SERVES 8

FOR THE MUSTARD SABAYON

½ cup plus 2 tsp. (4 ½ oz./125 g) Bresse butter

1 egg yolk

Scant ¼ cup (50ml) mineral water

½ tbsp. Madras curry mustard

FOR THE CURRY AND SHELLFISH MUSTARD

7 oz. (200 g) sauce américaine made from lobster and jumbo shrimp shells

⅓ cup plus 1 tbsp. (3 ½ oz./100 g) Madras curry mustard

1 pinch of Bresse or Espelette pepper

A few drops of lemon juice

Salt and freshly ground pepper

FOR THE RED CURRY SQUASH AND SHRIMPS

1 red kuri squash (6 inches/15 cm in diameter)

⅓ cup + 2 tbsp. (3 ½ oz./100 g) butter at room temperature

40 small brown shrimp

Oil for frying

A few Chinese chives

A drizzle of grapeseed or olive oil

¼ cup (1 oz./30 g) pumpkin seeds

Salt and freshly ground pepper

TO SERVE

A few strips of marinated ginger

A few wood sorrel and chickweed leaves

Chef's note

This dish was created last winter to showcase the red kuri squash grown by our market gardener Jérôme Gaudillère in Saint-Vincent-en-Bresse. The curry mustard brings out the flavors of the dish. It shouldn't dominate, but rather blend into the dish. The sabayon adds a contrasting sweetness to counterbalance the spicy glaze.

FOR THE MUSTARD SABAYON

In a saucepan, heat the butter until it turns a nutty color (*beurre noisette*). In a *bain-marie* (a mixing bowl placed in a pan of simmering water) whisk the egg yolk with the mineral water until frothy, then add the *beurre noisette* and the mustard.
Pour into a whipped cream dispenser with two cartridges and place in a *bain-marie*.

FOR THE CURRY AND SHELLFISH MUSTARD

In a saucepan, reduce the sauce américaine until it has a syrupy consistency. Leave to cool.
In a mixing bowl, mix the mustard, Bresse or Espelette pepper, lemon juice, and the reduced sauce américaine. Season with salt and pepper. Refrigerate.

FOR THE RED CURRY SQUASH AND SHRIMPS

Preheat the oven to 325°F (160°C). Wash the squash well, cut in half, remove the seeds, and cut each half into four slices. In a mixing bowl, using a spatula, beat the butter until soft and creamy. Place the squash slices on a baking sheet and brush with the softened butter. Season with salt and pepper. Bake in the oven for 6 minutes. Just before serving, brush each squash slice with the curry and shellfish mustard, then bake for a further 5 minutes. Heat the oil in a deep fryer to 355°F (180°C), then fry the brown shrimp for 3 minutes. (To check that the oil is at the right temperature, throw a very small piece of bread into the fryer. When the crouton is golden, the oil is around 180°C.)
In a skillet, sauté the Chinese chives in the grapeseed or olive oil. Spread the pumpkin seeds out on a baking sheet. Bake at 325°F (160°C) for 10 minutes to make them puff up.

TO SERVE

Add a drop of curry and shellfish mustard to each plate and top with a squash slice. Divide the brown shrimp, Chinese chives, and wood-sorrel and chickweed leaves between the plates and decorate with a few strips of marinated ginger. Sprinkle with puffed pumpkin seeds and serve the mustard sabayon in individual pots.

LUCILE DAROSEY
LOISEAU DES DUCS
DIJON

MACAROON WITH HAZELNUT POWDER
AND BOURBON VANILLA MUSTARD

MAKES ABOUT 30 MACAROONS

FOR THE ITALIAN MERINGUE
½ cup (3 ½ oz./100 g) superfine sugar

2 ¼ tbsp. (33 ml) water

1 ¾ oz. (50 g) egg white
(about 1 ½ large whites)

FOR THE MACAROON MIXTURE
1 cup sifted (3 ¾ oz./110 g) confectioners' sugar

1 cup plus 2 tbsp. (3 ¾ oz./110 g) ground almonds

1 ¾ oz. (50 g) egg white
(about 1 ½ large whites)

1 tbsp. mustard seeds, coarsely ground

FOR THE MUSTARD GANACHE
2 ½ tbsp. whipping cream

1 tsp. (4 g) inverted sugar syrup (Trimoline)

1 tsp. (4 g) glucose

2 oz. (55 g) white chocolate, broken in pieces

3 ½ oz. (100 g) cold whipping cream

2 ½ tbsp. (1 ½ oz./40g) hazelnut powder
and Bourbon vanilla mustard

⅓ cup (2 ¾ oz./75 g) lemon curd

FOR THE ITALIAN MERINGUE
In a saucepan, heat the sugar and water to 245°F (118°C) and boil to obtain a syrup. Clean the sides of the pan regularly using a wet pastry brush to prevent sugar crystals from sticking to the sides. Whisk the egg whites in a food processor until just firm. Reduce the speed and drizzle in the syrup without it touching the whisk. Whip the egg whites until stiff and the meringue has cooled.

FOR THE MACAROON MIXTURE
Preheat the oven to 300°F (150°C). In a mixing bowl, stir together the confectioners' sugar and the ground almonds. Add the egg whites and fold in until the mixture is smooth. Stir in the meringue in two batches, then work the macaroon mixture using a spatula until it collapses slightly. Transfer the mixture to a pastry bag fitted with a ⅓ inch (8 mm) tip.
Pipe macaroons in staggered rows on baking sheets lined with paper baking liners. Sprinkle with the mustard seeds, then leave for about 30 minutes to form a crust. (The time may vary slightly depending on the humidity of the room.) Bake the macaroons for 15 minutes, then transfer them to a rack and leave to cool.

FOR THE MUSTARD GANACHE
In a saucepan, boil the 2 ½ tablespoons of whipping cream with the inverted sugar syrup and glucose. Pour the mixture over the white chocolate and stir to mix. Stir in the cold whipping cream and mustard, then refrigerate for at least 4 hours. Whisk the ganache then transfer it to a pastry bag.
Fill the cooled macarons with the ganache, adding the lemon curd in the center. Refrigerate the macaroons for 30 minutes before eating them to allow the flavors to blend perfectly.

Pastry Chef's note
I've chosen to use hazelnut powder and Bourbon mustard because of its very sophisticated flavor and the gourmet notes of Bourbon vanilla, which I particularly love. The hazelnut adds a woody, roasted flavor and the small grains of hazelnut "Cazette" flower are interesting in terms of texture, adding a little extra something to this whipped ganache! Finally, lemon curd lends its acidity and freshness to the macaroon.

OMAR DHIAB
LOISEAU RIVE GAUCHE
PARIS

MULLET MARINATED IN MADAGASCAR GREEN PEPPERCORN MUSTARD
WITH BROILED RED LEAF LETTUCE AND LOVAGE RELISH

SERVES 4

FOR THE GREEN PEPPERCORN-MARINATED MULLET
(prepare 48 hours in advance)

3 ½ oz. (100 g) shallots

¼ cup (1 ¾ oz./50 g) green peppercorns

2 tbsp. olive oil

Scant ¼ cup (50 ml) grapeseed oil

Scant ¼ cup (50 ml) extra virgin olive oil

2 cups (500 ml) lemon juice

2 ¼ lb. (1 kg) mullet fillets

Coarse salt

FOR THE LEEK PURÉE

4 leeks

2 tbsp. plus 2 tsp. (40 ml) olive oil

2 cups (500 ml) chicken bouillon

Salt

FOR THE LOVAGE RELISH

½ red onion

Scant ½ cup (100 ml) sherry vinegar

1 bunch of lovage

4 tsp. (20 ml) olive oil

1 egg

Grated zest of 1 lemon

Juice of ½ lemon

Cayenne pepper

Salt and freshly ground pepper

FOR THE FRIED ONIONS

4 green onions

⅓ cup (1 ¾ oz./50 g) all-purpose flour

1 scant cup (200 ml) groundnut oil

FOR THE GREEN PEPPERCORN-MARINATED MULLET

Prepare the marinade 48 hours in advance. Peel and finely chop the shallot. In a sauté pan, sweat the shallots and the green peppercorns in the 2 tablespoons of olive oil. Transfer to a bowl and mix together with the grape seed oil and extra virgin olive oil. Leave to cool in the refrigerator. Stir in the lemon juice, cover with plastic wrap, and chill for 48 hours.

Two hours before serving the dish, cover the mullet fillets with coarse salt and leave for 3 to 4 minutes, depending on their size, to tighten the flesh and season it thoroughly. Rinse the fillets and strain the marinade through a fine-mesh sieve. Place the mullet fillets in the green pepper marinade for 3 to 4 minutes, then set aside in the refrigerator.

FOR THE LEEK PURÉE

Clean the leeks, then finely chop the white part. In a sauté pan, sweat the leeks in the olive oil. Season with salt. Add the chicken bouillon and cook quickly to preserve the natural color of the leeks. Drain then blend to a purée. Strain through a fine-mesh sieve and set aside. The purée should be quite thick.

FOR THE LOVAGE RELISH

Peel and chop the onion as finely as possible. In a sauté pan, cook the onion with the sherry vinegar until all the liquid has evaporated. Set aside.

Pick the leaves from the lovage and crush half of them in a mortar, then blend in the olive oil. Alternatively, you can make this relish in a food processor. Finely chop the remainder of the lovage leaves.

Carefully lower the egg into a saucepan of boiling water and cook for 6 minutes to soft boil. Remove it with a slotted spoon and gently roll the egg on a work counter to crack the shell, then peel it under cold running water.

In a mixing bowl, stir together the leek purée, the soft-boiled egg, and the lovage relish. Blend, then stir in the chopped lovage leaves, the vinegared onion, and the lemon zest. Season to taste with lemon juice, cayenne pepper, salt, and freshly ground pepper.

FOR THE FRIED ONIONS

Slice the onions 1/16 inch (2 mm) thick on a mandoline. Dip them in the flour, then fry them immediately in the groundnut oil, heated to about 265°F (130°C).

FOR THE BROILED RED LEAF LETTUCE

1 red leaf lettuce

Olive oil

½ tsp. (2 g) anchovy powder

Freshly ground pepper

FOR THE MINI LEEKS WITH MUSTARD-HONEY VINAIGRETTE

1 tsp. Madagascar green peppercorn mustard

1 tsp. Burgundy mustard

1 tsp. olive oil

1 tsp. acacia honey

4 mini leeks

TO SERVE

4 grapefruit segments, halved

A few small sorrel and red oxalis leaves

FOR THE BROILED RED LEAF LETTUCE

Just before serving, cut the red leaf lettuce into quarters and season with a drizzle of olive oil. Cook under the oven broiler for 30 to 40 seconds. Remove from the oven and season with the anchovy powder, fried onions and freshly ground pepper.

FOR THE MINI LEEKS WITH MUSTARD-HONEY VINAIGRETTE

Blend the mustards, olive oil, and honey to make the vinaigrette. Cook the leeks in a large pan of boiling salted water for 10 minutes until tender. Cut them at an angle into 1 ½ inches (4 cm) lengths and marinate them in the vinaigrette.

TO SERVE

Brush the marinated mullet fillets with the remaining vinaigrette. Arrange the marinated mullet, leek purée, lovage relish, fried onions, broiled red leaf lettuce, and mini leeks in vinaigrette on each plate. Add the halved grapefruit segments and garnish with the sorrel and red oxalis. If you have any pieces of fried onion left, sprinkle them over the dish.

Chef's note

I'm particularly partial to Madagascar green peppercorns and they add a wonderful freshness to the marinated fish and leeks. Used here in a relish, this spice enhances the leek and gives it a more appetizing and original flavor.

RUBÉN ESCUDERO
MANKO
PARIS

BEEF HEART *ANTICUCHO*
WITH BURGUNDY AND BASIL MUSTARDS

SERVES 4

FOR THE VEGETABLES

4 ¼ oz. (120 g) Vitelotte
(small blue-violet) potatoes

4 ¼ oz. (120 g) new potatoes

Generous ½ cup (2 ¾ oz./80 g)
choclo (Peruvian corn)

1 tbsp. sugar

½ lemon

¾ oz. (20 g) *ají amarillo*
(Peruvian yellow chile pepper)

¼ cup (2 ¼ oz. /60 g) butter

4 tsp. (¾ oz./20 g)
basil white wine Dijon mustard

A few fresh cilantro leaves, thinly sliced

Fleur de sel de Guérande sea salt

Cracked black pepper

FOR THE PRESERVED *AJÍ AMARILLO*

1 ¼ cups (300 ml) sunflower oil

7 oz. (200 g) *ají amarillo*

⅓ cup (1 ½ oz./40 g) roughly
chopped white onion

⅓ cup (1 ½ oz./40 g) roughly
chopped red onion

2 garlic cloves, minced

FOR THE *ANTICUCHERA* MARINADE

200 g *ají panca* paste (chile paste)

½ tbsp. cracked black pepper

½ tsp. ground cumin

¼ cup (7 g) dried oregano

½ tbsp. salt

2 tbsp. red wine vinegar

1 small garlic clove, peeled

Scant ½ cup (100 ml) sunflower oil

11 ¼ oz. (320 g) beef heart

FOR THE *TARI* SAUCE

8 ¾ oz. (250 g) preserved *ají amarillo*

1 egg

2 tbsp. Burgundy mustard

3 g marigold leaves

Scant ½ cup (100 ml) sunflower oil

½ tsp. ground cumin

½ tsp. salt

TO FINISH

¼ tsp. cilantro sprouts

FOR THE VEGETABLES

Wash the potatoes, then steam them for about 30 minutes.
Cut them in half.
In a saucepan, simmer the corn with the sugar for about
10 minutes. Drain, then sprinkle with lemon juice to keep its
pretty color.
Wash the *ají amarillo*, then remove seeds and cut into thin strips.
In a skillet, heat the butter. Add the potatoes and corn and fry
until golden. Stir in the mustard. Remove from the heat and add
the chopped cilantro and the *ají amarillo*. Season with the sea salt
and crushed black pepper. Keep warm.

FOR THE PRESERVED *AJÍ AMARILLO*

In a skillet, heat the oil, then add the *ají amarillo*, onions, and
garlic. Cook over very low heat for 1 hour.

FOR THE *ANTICUCHERA* MARINADE

In a blender, mix all the ingredients except the sunflower oil.
Gradually drizzle in the oil without emulsifying. Coat the beef
heart with the marinade and set aside in the refrigerator.

FOR THE *TARI* SAUCE

In a blender, mix the preserved *ají amarillo* with the egg. Add
the mustard and the marigold leaves, then make the sauce as you
would mayonnaise, gradually drizzling in the oil until the mixture
thickens. Season with cumin and salt.

TO FINISH

Cut the beef heart into strips. In a skillet, sear the marinated beef
until cooked to your liking. Arrange some marinated beef heart
and hot vegetables on each plate. Add a few dots of *tari* sauce and
a little of the remaining preserved *ají amarillo*. Scatter over the
cilantro sprouts. Season to taste.

Chef's note
The two mustards chosen for this recipe
go perfectly with the strong flavors of
the marinade and the beef heart. Cooking
the potatoes slowly brings out the fresh
taste of the basil in the mustard, while
combining the Burgundy mustard with
the *tari* sauce brings out a fine fresh
aroma that distinguishes this dish from
the classic version.

RUBÉN ESCUDERO
MANKO
PARIS

OCTOPUS WITH OLIVES
AND PINOT NOIR MUSTARD

SERVES 4

FOR THE OCTOPUS
5 ¾ oz. (160 g) octopus
Coarse salt

FOR THE CRISPY BRIOCHE
1 ½ oz. (40 g) brioche (or 1 thick slice)
2 tbsp. butter

**FOR THE PINOT NOIR
MUSTARD MAYONNAISE**
⅔ cup (3 ½ oz./100 g) pitted
Kalamata black olives
1 egg
1 ¼ cups (300 ml) sunflower oil
2 ½ tbsp. Pinot noir mustard
½ lime

FOR THE BLACK OLIVE *CHIMICHURRI*
1 ½ tbsp. capers
Scant ½ tbsp. drained green peppercorns in
brine
1 tbsp. pitted black olives
½ tsp. minced garlic
Scant ¼ cup (50 ml) olive oil
4 tsp. Chardonnay vinegar
½ tbsp. honey
¼ cup (10 g) chopped parsley

TO FINISH
10 cherry tomatoes, cut in half
1 avocado, pitted, peeled and cut into strips
A few cilantro sprouts

Chef's note
The sweet and fragrant taste of
Pinot noir mustard goes well with
the octopus and black olive flavors in
this reinterpretation of a traditional
Peruvian recipe.

FOR THE OCTOPUS
Rinse the octopus in cold water while rubbing it with the coarse
salt. Repeat this process several times until the water runs clear
and the octopus is no longer slimy. Cut the octopus pieces into
strips and cook in a large covered pot of boiling water for about 20
minutes. Leave to stand in the cooking water for 10 minutes, still
covered. Drain, leave to cool, then refrigerate.

FOR THE CRISPY BRIOCHE
Cut the brioche into thin strips. In a skillet, clarify the butter, then
brown the brioche in this clarified butter. Transfer the brioche
onto paper towels to absorb excess fat.

FOR THE PINOT NOIR MUSTARD MAYONNAISE
Blend the black olives. Add the egg and mix in. Gradually drizzle
in the oil while continuing to blend. When the mixture begins
to thicken, add the mustard and lemon juice. Mix to obtain a
mayonnaise. Refrigerate.

FOR THE BLACK OLIVE *CHIMICHURRI*
Finely chop the capers, green peppercorns, black olives, and
garlic. Add the oil, vinegar, honey, and parsley and stir together.

TO FINISH
Arrange some octopus strips, cherry tomato halves, and avocado
slices on each plate. Season with a little black-olive *chimichurri*
and mustard mayonnaise. Divide the crispy brioche between the
plates and garnish with the cilantro sprouts.

TIRADITO BACHICHE
WITH HONEY AND BALSAMIC DIJON MUSTARD

SERVES 4

FOR THE FISH MARINATED IN *AJÍ AMARILLO*

⅓ cup (2 ¾ oz./80 g) *ají amarillo* paste

4 tsp. honey and balsamic Dijon mustard

¼ tsp. coriander seeds, crushed

11 ¼ oz. (320 g) lean white fish fillets
(eg seabream, mullet, or sea bass)

Salt

FOR THE PARMESAN CRISPS

1 cup (3 ½ oz./100 g) finely grated Parmesan

FOR THE PARMESAN *LECHE DE TIGRE*

3 ½ oz. (100 g) Parmesan rind

1 cup (3 ½ oz./100 g) finely grated Parmesan

⅓ oz. (10 g) white onion heart

1 ½ oz. (40 g) white fish scraps

⅓ cup (80 ml) lime juice (about 3 limes)

½ tsp. minced garlic

½ tsp. salt

4 g cilantro stalks

2 g Habanero chile pepper

TO FINISH

4 tsp. basil oil

4 tsp. balsamic vinegar

Some untreated lemon zest

A few basil sprouts

FOR THE FISH MARINATED IN *AJÍ AMARILLO*

To make the marinade, blend together the *ají amarillo* paste, mustard, and crushed coriander seeds. Spread over the fish fillets and leave to marinate in the fridge for 2 hours.

Drain the fish fillets and lightly salt them. Reserve the marinade. Using a spit or a hook, hang each fillet and quickly pass the flame of a hot blowtorch over the entire surface of the fish to lightly brown (tataki style), then immerse the fillets in iced water for 2 to 3 minutes to stop the cooking process. Transfer the fillets to paper towels and dry them.

Cut the marinated fish into ⅓–½ oz. (10–15 g) strips. Refrigerate.

FOR THE PARMESAN CRISPS

Form circles of grated Parmesan on the surface of a hot non-stick skillet and heat until they are lightly browned. Using a spatula, carefully transfer them to paper towels to remove excess fat.

If you want to give them a tuile shape, carefully mold them onto a rolling pin as soon as you remove them from the pan.

FOR THE PARMESAN *LECHE DE TIGRE*

Infuse a saucepan of water with the Parmesan rind for 45 minutes, without boiling. Strain the Parmesan water through a fine sieve and reserve ½ cup (120 ml). In a blender (preferably a glass one to prevent the lemon juice oxidizing), blend the grated Parmesan, reserved Parmesan water, onion, fish, lemon juice, garlic, and salt. Once the mixture is smooth, add the cilantro and the pepper, then quickly blend (pulsing two or three times at high speed) to flavor the *leche de tigre* without coloring it. Refrigerate.

TO FINISH

Drizzle lines of the reserved marinade on each plate. If you wish, you can then heat them with a blowtorch for a lightly smoked flavor. Divide the *leche de tigre* among the plates, then arrange the strips of marinated fish and the Parmesan crisps on top. Season with the basil oil and balsamic vinegar. Scatter over some lemon zest and basil sprouts and add a little salt, if necessary, before serving.

Chef's note

This mustard flavored with honey and balsamic vinegar adds a very refined taste that blends well with the *ají amarillo* without masking the taste of the fresh fish.

STRAWBERRY
WITH MUSTARD BRAN

SERVES 8

FOR THE STRAWBERRY SYRUP
(prepare the day before)
3 ½ oz. (100 g) strawberries
⅔ cup (150 ml) water
⅓ cup plus 1 tbsp. (2 ¾ oz./75 g) superfine sugar

FOR THE WHIPPED GANACHE
(prepare the day before)
5 ¾ oz. (160 g) white chocolate
½ cup (110 ml) hot whipping cream
2 tsp. seed style mustard
1 cup (100 ml) cold whipping cream
4 ½ tsp. (⅓ oz./10 g) mustard bran

FOR THE STRAWBERRY ICE CREAM
Scant ¼ cup (50 ml) water
5 tsp. (¾ oz./20 g) superfine sugar
1 ½ tbsp. (½ oz./13 g) glucose powder
¼ tsp. (1 g) stabilizer
½ cup (4 ¼ oz./120 g) strawberry purée

FOR THE STRAWBERRY MOUSSE
1 tbsp. plus 2 tsp. (1 oz./25 g) whipping cream
1 gelatin sheet
½ oz. (15 g) white chocolate
3 ½ tbsp. (1 ¾ oz./50 g) strawberry purée

FOR THE STRAWBERRY SYRUP
The day before, boil the strawberries, water, and sugar in a saucepan. Leave to cool then cover with plastic wrap and refrigerate for 24 hours. This syrup will be used for the stewed strawberries and strawberry jam.

FOR THE WHIPPED GANACHE
The day before, melt the white chocolate in a saucepan and pour over the hot cream. Mix well, then add the mustard. Stir in the cold cream and the mustard bran. Refrigerate for 24 hours.

FOR THE STRAWBERRY ICE CREAM
In a saucepan, heat the water, sugar, glucose, and stabilizer to 185°F (85°C) to make a syrup. Leave to cool, then pour over the strawberry purée and mix together. Pour the mixture into an ice cream maker and churn. Transfer to the freezer.

FOR THE STRAWBERRY MOUSSE
Whip the cream using an electric whisk. In a bowl, soften the gelatin in cold water, then at 95°F (35°C). In a saucepan, melt the white chocolate. Squeeze out the gelatin and mix together with the strawberry purée, melted white chocolate, and whipped cream. Pour the mixture into a container to a thickness of ½ inch (1 cm), then refrigerate for 3 hours. Cut into 8 rectangles of 3 inches (8 cm) long by 1 inch (2.5 cm) wide.

FOR THE STEWED STRAWBERRIES
Preheat the oven to 320°F (165°C). Place the whole strawberries onto a baking sheet. Brush them with the melted butter, sprinkle with the sugar, and cook in the oven for 4 to 5 minutes. Transfer them to the strawberry syrup (which will later be used for the strawberry jam).

FOR THE STEWED STRAWBERRIES

1 ¼ oz. (32 g) strawberries

4 tsp. melted butter

5 tsp. (¾ oz./20 g) superfine sugar

FOR THE STRAWBERRY JAM

4 ½ oz. (125 g) strawberries

3 ½ tbsp. (1 ½ oz./40 g) superfine sugar

Juice from stewed strawberries

FOR THE RED SHORTBREAD COOKIES

2 ½ tbsp. (1 ¼ oz./36 g) butter

⅓ tsp. salt

2 ½ tbsp. (¾ oz./20 g) confectioners' sugar

4 tsp. (¼ oz./7 g) ground almonds

A few drops of red food coloring

1 tbsp. beaten egg

FOR THE CHOCOLATE DECORATION

300 g white couverture chocolate chips

2 tsp. (¼ oz./6 g) mustard bran

TO SERVE

24 strawberries

Mustard bran

FOR THE STRAWBERRY JAM

Cut the strawberries into pieces, then cook them in a saucepan with the sugar and the strawberry syrup until this acquires a coating consistency.

FOR THE RED SHORTBREAD COOKIES

Preheat the oven to 325°F (165°C). In a mixing bowl, rub the butter into the confectioners' sugar, ground almonds, and salt. Mix in the food coloring and the beaten egg. Let the dough rest for 15 minutes, then roll it out to a thickness of ⅛ inch (3 mm). Cut it into 8 rectangles of 4 inches (10 cm) long by 1 ½ inches (3.5 cm) wide. Bake in the oven for 7 minutes.

FOR THE CHOCOLATE DECORATION

Melt the white chocolate, then spread it on a sheet of parchment paper. When the chocolate has hardened, cut out 8 rectangles of 4 inches (10 cm) long by 1 ¼ inches (3 cm) wide and 8 rectangles of 3 inches (7.5 cm) long by 1 inch (2.5 cm) wide.

TO SERVE

Just before serving, whip the ganache using an electric whisk until smooth and creamy. Spread a little strawberry jam onto each plate, then dress with a shortbread cookie, some stewed strawberries, a large rectangle of white chocolate, a rectangle of strawberry mousse, a small rectangle of white chocolate and some fresh strawberries. Top with the whipped ganache and a sprinkling of bran and place some strawberry ice cream alongside.

Chef's note

Seed style mustard retains all the distinctiveness of this condiment. The bran is subtle but potent, with spicy and floral notes.

MEDLEY OF VEGETABLES
WITH ALIGOTÉ BOUILLON AND MUSTARD BRAN

SERVES 8

FOR THE JERUSALEM ARTICHOKE PURÉE
(prepare the day before)
1 oz. (30 g) Jerusalem artichokes
Generous ¼ cup (1 ¾ oz./50 g)
slightly salted butter

FOR THE ALIGOTÉ BOUILLON
2 ¼ oz. (60 g) shallots
¼ cup (1 ¾ oz./50 g) butter
1 ¼ cups (300 ml) Aligoté wine
⅝ cup (150 ml) chicken bouillon
⅝ cup (150 ml) whipping cream
Salt and freshly ground pepper

FOR THE VEGETABLES
4 small celery sticks
8 white asparagus spears
24 small salad leaves
32 spinach leaves
32 small oyster mushrooms (Pomponnette)
2 tbsp. clarified butter
Olive oil

TO SERVE
1 kohlrabi
Baby red-veined sorrel, parsley,
lemon balm, and celery leaves
Olive oil
Fleur de sel sea salt
Mustard bran

FOR THE JERUSALEM ARTICHOKE PURÉE
The day before, peel the Jerusalem artichokes, cut them in quarters, then put them in a vacuum sealer bag with the butter. Cook them in a large pan of boiling salted water for 1 hour 30 minutes. Remove the Jerusalem artichokes from the bag, blend them, then place in a cheesecloth-lined sieve and leave to drain overnight.

FOR THE ALIGOTÉ BOUILLON
Peel and finely chop the shallots, then sweat them in a saucepan with 1 ½ tablespoons of the butter. Pour in the wine and reduce by half, then add the chicken bouillon. Stir in the cream and reduce slightly. Using an immersion blender, whisk in the remainder of the butter. Season with salt and pepper.

FOR THE VEGETABLES
Wash all the vegetables and peel the asparagus. In a saucepan, slowly roast the whole celery sticks in the clarified butter (insert the blade of a knife to check they're done). Roast the asparagus and oyster mushrooms with a drizzle of olive oil. Cook the salad leaves and spinach over a low heat with a little olive oil until crispy, being careful to retain their color.

TO SERVE
Using a mandoline, cut 32 kohlrabi shavings. Season them with olive oil and sea salt. Draw a comma on each plate with the Jerusalem artichoke purée, then arrange the different vegetables on top. Scatter over the kohlrabi shavings and the baby leaves, then sprinkle with mustard bran. Reheat the Aligoté bouillon and serve it separately.

Chef's note
In this vegetable recipe, the mustard bran adds subtle but potent and floral notes.

MOURAD HADDOUCHE
LOISEAU DES VIGNES
BEAUNE

MARINATED BROOK TROUT

WITH RADISH CHIPS, CAULIFLOWER PICKLES, AND DILL AND LEMON MUSTARD

SERVES 4

FOR THE MARINADE
4 fresh brook trout fillets
(about 1 ¾ oz./50 g each)
2 ½ tbsp. (1 ½ oz./40 g) salt
5 tsp. superfine sugar
¼ cup (1 ½ oz./40 g) yellow mustard seeds

**FOR THE CAULIFLOWER
AND RADISH PICKLES**
2 ¼ lb. (1 kg) cauliflower (broken into florets)
10 radishes
1 ⅔ cups (400 ml) white vinegar
1 cup (240 ml) hazelnut oil
A little grapefruit zest

FOR THE MUSTARD MAYONNAISE
1 egg yolk
4 tsp. (20g) dill and lemon mustard
2 tbsp. grapefruit juice
Scant ¼ cup (50 ml) hazelnut oil

TO SERVE
Fresh red caviar
A few watercress and borage sprouts
Hazelnut oil
A little grapefruit zest

FOR THE MARINADE
Rinse and dry the brook trout fillets. In a bowl, mix the salt, sugar, and mustard seeds, then cover the fillets with this marinade. Leave to marinate for 2 hours in the refrigerator to draw moisture out of the fish and firm the flesh.

FOR THE CAULIFLOWER AND RADISH PICKLES
Place the cauliflower in a pan of boiling salted water for 2 minutes to blanch it, then immerse it in a bowl of ice-cold water to prevent further cooking. Finely slice the radishes on a mandoline.
Place the cauliflower and radishes in separate bowls to keep the colors distinct. Heat the vinegar and pour it over the vegetables. Divide the hazelnut oil and the grapefruit zest between the two bowls. Set aside in the refrigerator.

FOR THE MUSTARD MAYONNAISE
Whisk together the egg yolk, mustard, and grapefruit juice. While continuing to whisk, gradually drizzle in the hazelnut oil to thicken the mayonnaise.

TO SERVE
Rinse the trout fillets well in cold water, dry them, then arrange on the plates. Cover them with a rosette of radish chips surrounded by the cauliflower pickles, red caviar, and watercress and borage sprouts. Dab some mustard mayonnaise around the plate, sprinkle the fillets with a dash of hazelnut oil and scatter over some grapefruit zest.

Chef's note
Dill and lemon mustard goes beautifully with fish, combining the freshness of dill with the acidity of white vinegar. The spiciness of the mustard seed and the clarity of the hazelnut oil add depth of flavor. You can serve this with one tablespoon of organic sheep cheese per person, served separately in a ramekin and seasoned with freshly ground pepper and a few mustard seeds.

COLIN LACH
MONSIEUR MOUTARDE
DIJON

L'AMOUR TARD
BURGUNDY VERJUICE

SERVES 1

FOR THE MUSTARD TINCTURE
(prepare the day before)
Makes 1 ½ cups/350 ml
1 ½ cups (350 ml) 120-proof (60° ABV) neutral spirit
Scant ½ cup (100 ml) mustard-seed oil

FOR THE COCKTAIL
Scant ¼ cup (50 ml) Compagnie des Indes® traditional aged rum
1 tbsp. sweet mead
1 tbsp. Menéres® 20 Years Old Tawny Port
2 tsp. Burgundy verjuice
20 drops of mustard tincture (see recipe above)
Ice, to shake

TO FINISH
Some untreated orange peel

FOR THE MUSTARD TINCTURE
The day before, mix together the alcohol and oil in an airtight container.
Leave to macerate for 4 hours, stirring every 30 minutes.
Place the container in the freezer and leave overnight.
Strain the contents through a coffee filter to separate the frozen oil from the alcohol, which will have been infused with the flavors of the oil.
Transfer the mustard tincture to a dropper bottle.

FOR THE COCKTAIL
Pour the rum into a pre-chilled cocktail shaker, followed by the sweet mead, port, verjuice and mustard tincture.
Fill three quarters full with ice cubes, then shake for about 20 seconds. Strain the cocktail into a previously chilled Champagne coupe.

TO FINISH
Peel some strips of orange peel and squeeze into the cocktail.
Cut some more pieces of peel to decorate the glass.

Head bartender's note
Mustard and honey—a classic association in the culinary world—are used here to highlight the complexity of the ingredients in this elaborate, dry, and aromatic cocktail. The verjuice adds balance, as well as a fresh and fruity touch that contrasts with the aromas of cooked fruit in the port, the pastry and exotic fruit notes of the rum, and the sweetness of the mead. The mustard tincture adds a subtle background texture that rounds off the flavors to a T.

COLIN LACH
MONSIEUR MOUTARDE
DIJON

L'AMOUR TARDE
BROWN MUSTARD SEEDS

SERVES 1

FOR THE MUSTARD SEED LIQUOR
(prepare 1 week in advance)
Makes 2 cups/500 ml

¼ cup (1 ½ oz./40 g) brown mustard seeds

12 Sarawak black peppercorns

1 ⅔ cups (400 ml) 100-proof (50° ABV) neutral spirit

5 tbsp. (75 ml) water

⅓ cup plus 1 tbsp. (2 ¾ oz./75 g) sugar

FOR THE COCKTAIL

2 ½ tbsp. Armagnac Castarède® VSOP

4 tsp. homemade mustard-seed liquor (see recipe above)

4 tsp. Río Viejo Oloroso Sherry

1 tbsp. lemon juice

2 tsp. cane sugar syrup

5 tsp. (23 g) egg white

Ice, to shake

TO FINISH

A few mustard seeds

1 dried lemon slice

FOR THE MUSTARD SEED LIQUOR

Macerate the mustard seeds and black peppercorns in the neutral spirit for six days. Filter the contents through a coffee filter to separate the seeds from the alcohol. In a saucepan, heat the water and sugar over a low heat to make a syrup. Leave to cool. Mix the mustard-macerated alcohol with the syrup. Bottle the mustard seed liquor.

FOR THE COCKTAIL

Pour the Armagnac into a cocktail shaker, followed by the mustard-seed liquor, sherry, lemon juice, cane sugar syrup and egg white. Shake vigorously without ice (this technique is known as dry shaking) then fill the shaker three quarters full with ice cubes and shake a second time. Fill a chilled tumbler with ice cubes then strain the cocktail into the glass.

TO FINISH

Decorate with mustard seeds and a dried lemon slice.

Head bartender's note
Inspired by Fallot's fine walnut Dijon mustard, this cocktail is delicious, voluptuous and tangy. The mustard seed liquor gives it a strong aromatic presence, while the Oloroso Sherry adds oxidative notes that recall the nuttiness of walnuts and blend perfectly with the Armagnac. The lemon juice, cane sugar syrup and egg white meanwhile give the cocktail its balance and texture.

CHRISTOPHE MULLER
PAUL BOCUSE
COLLONGES-AU-MONT-D'OR

COD WITH "SOUFFLÉED" PAPRIKA MUSTARD

SERVES 4

FOR THE COD
4 cod steaks with skin
Olive oil

FOR THE PAPRIKA MUSTARD
⅓ cup plus 1 tbsp. (3 ½ oz./100 g) Burgundy mustard
2 tbsp. peanut oil
4 tsp. olive oil
1 pinch of paprika

FOR THE COD
In a hot skillet, briefly sear the cod steaks in a drizzle of olive oil. Keep them warm.

FOR THE PAPRIKA MUSTARD
In a large bowl, whisk the mustard, while gradually drizzling in the peanut oil. Continue to whisk, as you would to make a mayonnaise, while drizzling in the olive oil. Stir in the paprika.

TO FINISH
Preheat the oven to 360°F (180°C). Carefully place the cod steaks, skin side up, in a baking dish. Cover with a generous layer of the paprika mustard. Bake for a few minutes: the fish will finish cooking and the mustard will "soufflé" slightly.

Chef's note
The mustard puffs up in the heat, forming a kind of crust, and its taste becomes milder. You can also use this paprika mustard to coat seared chicken thighs, pork ribs, or a ham.

CHRISTOPHE MULLER
PAUL BOCUSE
COLLONGES-AU-MONT-D'OR

MONSIEUR PAUL'S RUSSIAN-STYLE CUCUMBER
WITH DIJON MUSTARD

SERVES 4

1 lb. 2 oz. (500 g) cucumber (about 2 large)

4 tsp. (20 g) salt

⅓ cup plus 1 ½ tbsp. (100 g) heavy cream

4 tsp. Dijon mustard

1 tbsp. chopped dill

½ lemon

Slices of toast, to serve

Peel the cucumber and cut it in half lengthwise. Using a spoon, remove the seeds. Slice the cucumber into thin slices, then place them in a bowl. Cover with the salt, mix well, and leave for 2 hours. The salt will soften the cucumber.

Rinse the cucumber under cold water and drain it by squeezing between your hands.

In a bowl, mix together the cream, mustard, and dill, then add a few drops of lemon juice. Pour this sauce over the cucumber and stir together.

Serve the Russian-style cucumber with slices of toast.

Chef's note

Monsieur Paul liked to eat Russian-style cucumber with toasted baguette to accompany leftover stew. You could also enjoy it with salmon, or a scallop tartare. According to Paul Bocuse, you need strong-tasting mustard seeds. At the time, there were fewer variations of flavored mustards available, so Dijon mustard became the standard.

PORK TENDERLOIN
WITH DIJON MUSTARD "PÉPÉ FRITZ" SAUCE

SERVES 4

FOR THE PORK TENDERLOIN
1 pork tenderloin (about 1 lb. 5 oz./600 g)

FOR THE "PÉPÉ FRITZ" SAUCE
1 onion, finely chopped
½ cup (120 ml) dry white wine
1 tbsp. Dijon mustard
½ tbsp. tomato paste
⅔ cup (100 g) heavy cream

FOR THE PORK TENDERLOIN
In a skillet, sear the pork tenderloin on each side. Remove the meat from the pan, reserving the pork fat in the pan, and keep it warm.

FOR THE "PÉPÉ FRITZ" SAUCE
Sauté the onion until golden in the fat remaining in the skillet, then deglaze the pan with the white wine and reduce until all the liquid has evaporated.
Add the mustard and tomato paste to the pan, then mix with a whisk. Once the sauce has turned orange, add the cream and quickly whisk it in.

TO FINISH
Slice the pork tenderloin and serve with the Dijon mustard "Pépé Fritz" sauce.

Chef's note
I have my grandfather, a great cook, to thank for this recipe. In his day, refrigerators always contained mustard, white wine, tomato paste, and crème fraîche. When I was little, he would make this "Pépé Fritz" sauce as an accompaniment to a veal cutlet or chicken— it's a classic sauce from my childhood!

AYMERIC PINARD
LA CÔTE D'OR
SAULIEU

MANDARIN WITH DIJON MUSTARD,
PARFAIT GLACÉ, MANDARIN CONFIT AND MUSTARD FOAM

SERVES 4

FOR THE MANDARIN JELLY

75 g mandarin juice

2 g NH pectin

3 tbsp. (35 g) superfine sugar

0.5 g citric acid

0.5 g gelatin powder

FOR THE MANDARIN CONFIT

4 ½ oz. (125 g) mandarins, peeled and sliced

1 cup (250 ml) water

1 ¼ cups (8 ¾ oz./250 g) superfine
(caster) sugar

¾ oz. (20 g) mandarin segments, chopped

2 strips of mandarin zest

1 strip of lemon zest

FOR THE PARFAITS GLACÉS

1 tbsp. superfine sugar

½ tsp. water

⅓ oz. (10 g) egg white

1 g gelatin powder

¼ cup (60 ml) mandarin juice

¼ cup plus 2 tsp. (35 ml)
whipping cream

FOR THE MANDARIN COULIS

1 cup (250 ml) mandarin juice

¾ tbsp. (7.5 g) cornstarch

FOR THE MANDARIN JELLY

In a saucepan, heat the mandarin juice to 122°F (50°C), then add the pectin and sugar. Bring to a boil then stir in the citric acid and gelatin powder. Pour a third of the mixture into a rimmed baking sheet to a thickness of 1/12 inch (2.5 mm). Reserve the remainder of the mixture for the mandarin confit. Leave to set in the refrigerator for 15 minutes. Cut out 1 ½ inches (4 cm) discs from the jelly.

FOR THE MANDARIN CONFIT

Blanch the mandarin slices three times in a pot of boiling water then drain. Pour the 1 cup (250 ml) water into another saucepan and add the mandarin slices and half the sugar. Leave to poach gently for about 1 hour 30 minutes, ensuring that the temperature does not rise above 158°F (70°C).
At the end of cooking, add the remainder of the sugar to concentrate the syrup. Remove the mandarin slices from the syrup, let them cool, then chop finely.
Whip the reserved mandarin jelly, then stir in the chopped mandarin segments, the chopped mandarin confit, and the mandarin and lemon zest. Refrigerate.

FOR THE PARFAITS GLACÉS

Make an Italian meringue: in a saucepan, cook the sugar with the water at 244°F (118°C), then quickly pour the syrup over the egg whites. Whisk lightly by hand, then continue using an electric whisk until completely cooled.
Dissolve the gelatin in a little heated mandarin juice, then pour in the remaining juice. Whip the cream using an electric whisk. Gently stir together the Italian meringue, the jellified mandarin juice, and the whipped cream. Pour the mixture into silicone half-sphere molds to make half mandarins and freeze for 3 hours.

FOR THE MANDARIN COULIS

Put the mandarin juice and cornstarch into a saucepan and bring to a low boil. Stir and leave to thicken. Refrigerate.

FOR THE MUSTARD FOAM

4 tbsp. water

⅓ cup (2 ¼ oz./60 g) superfine sugar

3 g agar-agar

2 ½ tbsp. (¾ oz./22 g) gelatin powder

⅓ cup plus ½ tbsp. (3 ¼ oz./90 g) Dijon mustard

3 cups plus 3 tbsp. (750 ml) mandarin juice

½ cup (120 ml) lemon juice

FOR THE SWEET PIE DOUGH

¾ cup sifted (2 ¾ oz./75 g) confectioners' sugar

¼ cup (1 oz./25 g) ground almonds

½ cup plus 1 tsp. (4 ¼ oz./120 g) slightly salted butter

2 egg yolks

FOR THE MUSTARD FOAM

In a saucepan, boil the water and sugar with the agar-agar. Add the gelatin, then pour over the mustard and citrus juices. Mix and pour into a siphon fitted with two cartridges. Refrigerate.

FOR THE SWEET PIE DOUGH

Preheat the oven to 300°F (150°C). In a food processor, mix all the ingredients until you have a sweet pie dough. Using a rolling pin, roll out the dough between two sheets of parchment paper, then cut out 2 ¼ inches (5.5 cm) diameter discs. Arrange the discs on a baking sheet covered with a silicone sheet and bake for 12 minutes.

TO SERVE

Pour a little mandarin coulis into each deep dessert plate. Turn out the parfaits glacés and arrange them on the coulis. Using a spoon, gently form a hollow in the parfaits to allow space for a little mandarin confit.

Place a disc of mandarin jelly on each circle of sweet pie crust. Using a knife, draw lines from the center of the jelly discs outward to look like mandarin segments, then place the discs on the parfaits.

Using the siphon, place the foam into small containers to serve as a seasoning.

Pastry Chef's note

Mustard is rarely used in desserts but goes beautifully here with the tangy note of mandarin.

JUMBO SHRIMP WITH PURPLE ARTICHOKES,
PICKLED RED ONION, AND DIJON MUSTARD AND LEMON VERBENA SABAYON

SERVES 4

FOR THE JUMBO SHRIMP
8 langoustines
2 tbsp. olive oil
Salt and freshly ground pepper

FOR THE DIJON MUSTARD AND LEMON VERBENA SABAYON
1 ½ egg yolks
1 whole egg
2 tsp. Dijon mustard
½ tsp. salt
½ tsp. sherry vinegar
5 tsp. olive oil
Scant ½ cup (100 ml) lemon verbena oil

FOR THE PICKLED RED ONION
½ red onion
⅓ cup (80 ml) red wine vinegar
Scant ¼ cup (50 ml) water
5 tsp. (¾ oz./20 g) sugar
⅓ bay leaf

FOR THE PURPLE ARTICHOKES
2 purple artichokes
Juice of 1 lemon
1 ¾ oz. (50 g) onion (about ⅓ cup plus 1 tbsp. finely chopped)
¾ oz. (20 g) carrots (about 2 tbsp. finely chopped)
1 garlic clove
2 tbsp. olive oil
Scant ¼ cup (50 ml) white wine
Scant 1 cup (200 ml) water
1 thyme sprig
Salt and freshly ground pepper

TO FINISH
Some lemon marmalade

FOR THE JUMBO SHRIMP
Preheat the broiler. Shell the shrimp and place on a baking sheet. Season with salt and pepper. Brush the shrimp with olive oil and cook under the broiler for 1 minute.

FOR THE DIJON MUSTARD AND LEMON VERBENA SABAYON
In a mixing bowl, whisk together all the ingredients. Strain the mixture through a fine sieve, then pour into a siphon with two cartridges. Place the siphon in a *bain-marie* at 130°F (55°C).

FOR THE PICKLED RED ONION
Peel the onion and separate the layers to obtain petals. In a saucepan, boil the wine vinegar, water, and sugar. Add the bay leaf and onion petals and leave to infuse for 2 hours. Drain and set aside in the refrigerator.

FOR THE PURPLE ARTICHOKES
Prepare the artichokes and cut them into quarters. Place in a bowl of water with the lemon juice. Finely chop the onion, carrot, and garlic, then, sweat them in olive oil in a saucepan. Add the artichokes, season with salt and pepper and sweat again. Deglaze with the white wine and reduce until all the liquid has evaporated. Add the water and thyme, cover, and simmer for 20 minutes. Remove the artichokes and set aside.

TO FINISH
On each plate, arrange two shrimp, two artichoke quarters, two pieces of pickled onion, and a little lemon marmalade. Add some of the Dijon mustard and lemon verbena sabayon, then serve immediately.

Chef's note
I like to use Dijon mustard for its taste, its long finish, and its finesse, which perfectly balances the lemon verbena.

ÉRIC PRAS
MAISON LAMELOISE
CHAGNY-EN-BOURGOGNE

LINE-CAUGHT MACKEREL
WITH A SORREL MOUSSE TOPPING AND DIJON MUSTARD ICE CREAM

SERVES 4

FOR THE MACKEREL
1 mackerel (about 10 ½ oz./300 g)
Scant ½ cup (103 ½ oz./100 g) coarse gray salt
Espelette pepper
4 tsp. olive oil

FOR THE SORREL MOUSSE
2 cups (500 ml) whole milk
¾ oz. (20 g) gelatin leaves
3 sorrel leaves

FOR THE MACKEREL BOUILLON
Mackerel bones and trimmings (see above)
4 tsp. olive oil
1 ¾ oz. (50 g) shallots (about ¼ cup finely chopped)
1 garlic clove
1 thyme sprig
Scant ¼ cup (50 ml) white wine
2 tbsp. soy sauce
1 ⅔ cups (400 ml) mineral water

FOR THE DIJON MUSTARD ICE CREAM
½ cup (120 ml) whole milk
½ cup (120 ml) whipping cream
1 g stabilizer (optional)
3 g gelatin leaves
2 ½ tbsp. Dijon mustard

TO FINISH
A few red sorrel leaves
Ground roasted hazelnuts

FOR THE MACKEREL
Lift the mackerel fillets and remove any small bones. Reserve the bones and trimmings. Cover the fillets with coarse salt and leave for 5 minutes, then rinse and dry with paper towels. Sprinkle the fillets with Espelette pepper, brush them on the skin side with olive oil, and roll them up in dampened paper towels. Cook them in an oven on steam mode set at 150°F (65°C) (or use an electric steam cooker). Remove them when the core temperature has reached 113°F (45°C). Let cool.

FOR THE SORREL MOUSSE
Boil the milk in a saucepan. Soak the gelatin sheets in a bowl of water for 5 to 10 minutes until soft, then wring them out. Strain the milk into a bowl through a fine-mesh sieve, add the gelatin leaves, and stir in. Leave the mixture to set in the refrigerator for 1 hour, then pour into a food processor fitted with a whisk attachment and emulsify. Cut the sorrel leaves into tiny squares, then add them to the mixture. Coat the mackerel fillets with this mousse. Leave to set in the refrigerator for 15 minutes.

FOR THE MACKEREL BOUILLON
Crush the mackerel bones and cut the trimmings into large pieces. Heat the olive oil in a sauté pan, then add the fish bones and trimmings and brown. Peel and finely chop the shallots. Peel the garlic. Add the shallots, garlic, and thyme to the pan, then continue cooking. Deglaze with the white wine and reduce until all the liquid has evaporated. Deglaze with the soy sauce. Add the water and simmer for 25 minutes. Strain through a fine-mesh sieve and reduce slightly. Leave to cool.

FOR THE DIJON MUSTARD ICE CREAM
In a saucepan, boil the milk and cream. Add the stabilizer. Soak the gelatin leaves in a bowl of water for 5 to 10 minutes until soft, then wring them out and add them to the cream mixture. Strain through a fine-mesh sieve and, when the mixture is lukewarm, stir in the mustard. Churn in an ice cream maker.

TO FINISH
Cut the mackerel fillets into eight equal-size pieces. Arrange two pieces of mackerel on each plate, top with a few sorrel leaves and sprinkle with ground toasted hazelnuts. Add a quenelle of mustard ice cream and surround with a drizzle of the cold mackerel bouillon.

Chef's note
In this recipe, the Dijon mustard in the ice cream adds finesse and a spiciness that enhances all the flavors.

ÉRIC PRAS
MAISON LAMELOISE
CHAGNY-EN-BOURGOGNE

ROAST SADDLE OF RABBIT
WITH CELERY RAVIOLI, MUSSELS, GRAVY, AND SEED STYLE MUSTARD

SERVES 4

FOR THE SADDLE OF RABBIT
2 saddles of free-range rabbit
4 celery stalks
Scant ¼ cup (50 ml) olive oil
4 tsp. (¾ oz./20 g) butter
Salt and freshly ground pepper

FOR THE RABBIT GRAVY
2 tbsp. olive oil
1 carrot, peeled and cut into pieces
1 thyme sprig
3 tbsp. soy sauce
1 ⅔ cups (400 ml) water
¼ cup (1 ¾ oz./50 g) butter
2 tbsp. seed style mustard

FOR THE CELERY RAVIOLI
14 oz. (400 g) celery root (celeriac)
2 tbsp. olive oil
¼ cup (⅓ oz./10 g) snipped chives
1 tsp. seed style mustard
Salt and freshly ground pepper

FOR THE COATED MUSSELS
5 oz. (150 g) Bouchot mussels
1 shallot
1 garlic clove
4 tsp. olive oil
Scant ½ cup (100 ml) white wine
Scant ½ cup (100 ml) water
1 thyme sprig
0.5 g kappa carrageenan
(vegetable gelling agent)

TO FINISH
8 celery leaves in tempura (optional)

Chef's note
I have chosen to use seed style mustard, which I "toast" with *beurre noisette* to fix its aromas – its graininess gives a pleasing crunch to the rabbit gravy.

FOR THE SADDLE OF RABBIT
Bone the saddles of rabbit and cut each one half. Reserve the belly skin, bones and trimmings. Season the fillets with salt and pepper. Peel the celery and blanch it. Place a celery stalk against each fillet, wrap in a piece of the belly skin, and secure with string. In a casserole dish, roast the saddles of rabbit in the olive oil and butter for about 7 minutes. Leave to rest for 7 minutes. Remove the string and cut each half-saddle into three pieces.

FOR THE RABBIT GRAVY
Crush the rabbit bones and cut the trimmings into large pieces. In a casserole dish, brown the bones and trimmings in olive oil, then add the carrot and thyme. Deglaze with the soy sauce. Leave to caramelize, then pour in the water and cook over low heat for 30 minutes. Strain the gravy through a fine-mesh sieve, then reduce in a small saucepan. In a frying pan, brown the butter to make *beurre noisette*. Stir in the mustard and let it brown. Pour in the rabbit gravy and stir. Keep warm.

FOR THE CELERY RAVIOLI
Using a mandolin, cut half the celery root (celeriac) into eight thin slices, then cut out discs using a cookie cutter. Blanch them, immediately immerse in ice water, then drain them.
Finely chop the remainder of the celery root. Heat the olive oil in a saucepan and sweat the chopped celery root. Season with salt and pepper. Once the celery root is cooked, stir in the mustard and chives. Make into ravioli with the celery root discs.

FOR THE MUSSELS
Scrub and wash the mussels. Peel and finely chop the shallot and garlic, then sweat them in the olive oil in a casserole dish. Add the mussels and stir using a slotted spoon. Pour in the white wine and water and add the thyme. Cook, covered, for a few minutes until the mussels have opened. Strain and reserve the cooking juices. Remove the mussels from their shells.
Boil a scant ½ cup (100 ml) of the mussel cooking liquid with the kappa. Dip the mussels into the liquid one at a time using a wooden toothpick. Set aside.

TO FINISH
Reheat the ravioli in a steamer. Arrange three pieces of rabbit, two ravioli, two mussels, and two celery leaves in tempura (if using) on each plate. Add a little of the gravy.

GUILLAUME QUENZA AND MATTHIEU BIRON
FRÉQUENCE
PARIS

JAÏS

WHITE WINE VINEGAR

SERVES 1

FOR THE PEAR PICKLE VINEGAR
(prepare 4 days in advance)

2 ¼ lb. (1 kg) untreated pears

1 ⅔ cups (400 ml) white wine vinegar

1 ⅔ cups (400 ml) water

2 cups (14 oz./400 g) superfine sugar

8 g dried raspberry leaves

FOR THE ROASTED BUCKWHEAT TEA

Generous ½ cup (3 ½ oz./100 g) roasted buckwheat

2 cups (500 ml) boiling water

FOR THE COCKTAIL

2 tbsp. pear pickle vinegar
(see recipe above)

2 tbsp. Japanese whiskey

Scant ⅓ cup (70 ml) roasted buckwheat tea
(see recipe above)

Ice, to serve

Soda machine

FOR THE PEAR PICKLE VINEGAR

Cut the pears in half. In a saucepan, heat the wine vinegar, water, sugar, and raspberry leaves over low heat, stirring gently to dissolve the sugar. Add the pears and turn up the heat until the liquid boils. Remove from the heat and leave to cool. Refrigerate for 2 hours.
Strain and reserve the vinegar. The pears can be eaten as a dessert or sliced with a mandolin and dried.

FOR THE ROASTED BUCKWHEAT TEA

Infuse the boiling water with the roasted buckwheat for 5 minutes. Leave to cool.

FOR THE COCKTAIL

Mix the pear pickle vinegar, whiskey, and roasted buckwheat tea, then carbonate the cocktail using a soda machine. Serve immediately over ice.

Bartenders' note
Cooking will trigger the exchange between the juice in the pears and the white wine vinegar. The acidity of the vinegar will conserve the fruits during maceration. Vinegar is particularly appropriate here, serving as a perfect match for the freshness of the pear. Its acidity balances the sugar in the fruit while enhancing the taste of the whiskey.

GUILLAUME QUENZA AND MATTHIEU BIRON
FRÉQUENCE
PARIS

THÉO
BURGUNDY VERJUICE

SERVES 1

FOR THE *MATE* AND DRIED LIME SYRUP

2 dried limes

4 tsp. (¾ oz./20 g) *mate*

4 cups (1 L) boiling water

5 cups (2 ¼ lb./1 kg) superfine sugar

FOR THE COCKTAIL

1 tbsp. Burgundy verjuice

4 tsp. (20 ml) *mate* and dried lime syrup
(see recipe above)

2 ½ tbsp. Calvados

2 tsp. Suze

1 to 2 tbsp. sparkling water

Ice, to serve

FOR THE MATE AND DRIED LIME SYRUP

Mix the dried limes and the *mate* with the boiling water. Leave to cool at room temperature for 30 minutes. Strain, then stir in the sugar.

FOR THE COCKTAIL

Pour the verjuice into a shaker, followed by the mate and dried lime syrup, calvados and Suze. Mix vigorously, then add the sparkling water. Serve the cocktail over ice in a wine glass.

Bartenders' note

The verjuice adds an acidity that counterbalances the sweetness of the *mate* and dried lime syrup. Less aggressive than lemon, verjuice doesn't drown out the flavors and acts here as a link between the fruity notes of the calvados and the bitterness of gentian. Its delicate grape notes bring out the subtle aromas of the *mate* and dried lime while acidifying the cocktail and giving it a long finish that showcases the other aromas.

SYLVAIN SENDRA
FLEUR DE PAVÉ
PARIS

STEAMED COD
WITH SOY-BRAISED CABBAGE,
RAW CABBAGE, AND BURGUNDY MUSTARD SABAYON

SERVES 4

FOR THE STEAMED COD AND CABBAGE

4 cod steaks

7 oz. (200 g) Savoy cabbage and napa cabbage

4 tsp. soy sauce

8 pointed (hispi) cabbage leaves

1 lemon

Olive oil

FOR THE MUSTARD SABAYON

¼ cup (1 ¾ oz./50 g) butter, diced

12 egg yolks

2 tsp. (10 ml) water

4 tbsp. Burgundy mustard

FOR THE STEAMED COD AND THE CABBAGE

Steam the cod steaks for 3 minutes, rest them for 3 minutes under a sheet of foil.

Chop the savoy and napa cabbages, then cook in a sauté pan for a few minutes with a drizzle of olive oil. Stir the soy sauce into the cabbage. Cut the pointed cabbage leaves in half lengthwise, then season with the lemon juice and a drizzle of olive oil.

FOR THE MUSTARD SABAYON

Melt the butter. In a bowl, mix the egg yolks with 2 teaspoons of water, then place the bowl in a *bain-marie* to warm the mixture. Add the mustard and whisk briskly. Gradually whisk in the melted butter. Set aside.

TO FINISH

Arrange the cod, cooked cabbage, and raw cabbage on the plates. Drizzle over the mustard sabayon.

Chef's note

Burgundy mustard adds flavor, an attractive deep-yellow color, and a nice smooth texture.

SYLVAIN SENDRA
FLEUR DE PAVÉ
PARIS

RACK OF LAMB WITH DIJON MUSTARD
MASHED POTATO AND MIDDLE EASTERN SPICES

SERVES 4

FOR THE RACK OF LAMB
1 rack of lamb (8 ribs)
Salt and freshly ground pepper

FOR THE MUSTARD MASH
1 lb. 5 oz. (600 g) large floury potatoes
Scant ½ cup (100 ml) whole milk
¼ cup (1 ¾ oz./50 g) butter, diced
2 tsp. Dijon mustard
Salt

TO FINISH
Pinch za'atar
Pinch ground sumac
Pinch curry powder

FOR THE RACK OF LAMB
Season the rack of lamb with salt and pepper, then cook it whole, covered with foil, on the barbecue or in an oven preheated to 360°F (180°C) for 15 minutes.

FOR THE MUSTARD MASHED POTATO
Peel and wash the potatoes. Cook them in a large pan of boiling salted water for 25 minutes. Bring the milk to a boil in a small saucepan. Drain the potatoes and mash them with a potato masher. Add the butter, then pour in the hot milk, while continuing to mash. Stir in the mustard. Keep the mashed potato warm.

TO FINISH
Carve the rack of lamb and serve it with the mustard mashed potato. Sprinkle with spices and serve immediately.

Chef's note
Dijon mustard gives a kick to the mashed potato and works wonder for rejuvenating the taste buds!

SYLVAIN SENDRA
FLEUR DE PAVÉ
PARIS

MACKEREL *CEVICHE*
WITH SPICY CARPACCIO AND SEED STYLE DIJON MUSTARD

SERVES 4

FOR THE MACKEREL *CEVICHE*

2 boneless mackerel fillets, skin on

Juice of 1 lemon

Salt and freshly ground pepper

FOR THE SPICY CARPACCIO

1 horseradish

1 Green Meat radish

1 Red Meat radish

TO FINISH

⅓ cup plus 1 tbsp. (3 ½ oz./100 g)
seed style mustard

1 lemon

Olive oil

Aromatic herbs, finely chopped (eg dill, mint,
chervil, Thai basil)

Salt and freshly ground pepper

FOR THE MACKEREL *CEVICHE*

Cut the mackerel fillets into ¼ inch (0.5 cm) cubes, then marinate them in the lemon juice. Season with salt and pepper. Set aside in the refrigerator.

FOR THE SPICY CARPACCIO

Peel the horseradish. Using a mandolin, cut the horseradish and radishes into ⅛ inch (0.3 cm) thick slices. If you wish, you can then cut these slices into equal-size discs—or petals—using a cookie cutter.

TO FINISH

Using a paintbrush, draw lines of mustard over the surface of each (preferably white) plate. Arrange the carpaccio slices, alternating the colors as you go, then gently place the mackerel on top. Sprinkle with lemon juice and drizzle with olive oil. Season with salt and pepper and sprinkle with chopped herbs.

Chef's note

I love seed style mustard! The seeds add texture and the mustard's spiciness gives the dish extra punch.

KEISHI SUGIMURA
LE BÉNATON
BEAUNE

MUSTARD-BRAN MERINGUE BALLS
WITH BLACKCURRANT MUSTARD RED BERRIES AND MASCARPONE ICE CREAM

SERVES 6

FOR THE MERINGUES
3 ½ oz. (100 g) egg white (about 3 whites)

1 ½ cups sifted (5 oz./150 g) confectioners' sugar

⅔ cup (1 ¼ oz./35 g) mustard bran

FOR THE MASCARPONE ICE CREAM
Scant 1 cup (200 ml) whipping cream

5 egg yolks

Scant ¼ cup (50 ml) water

½ cup plus 2 tbsp. (4 ¼ oz./120 g) superfine sugar

⅔ cup (150 g/5 ¼ oz) mascarpone

FOR THE STRAWBERRY JELLY
10 ½ oz. (300 g) strawberries

2 ½ tbsp. (1 oz./30 g) superfine sugar

1 gelatin sheet

TO SERVE
10 ½ oz. (300 g) red berries

2 tbsp. (1 oz./30 g) blackcurrant and white wine Dijon mustard

4 tsp. (20 ml) reduced balsamic vinegar

A few seasonal red berries

FOR THE MERINGUES
Preheat the oven to 160°F (70°C). In a mixing bowl, whisk the egg whites, gradually pouring in the confectioner's sugar, then mix in the mustard bran. Place small dollops of the meringue into 12 half-sphere molds. Using the back of a spoon, smooth the meringue up the sides of the molds. Bake for about 5 hours.

FOR THE MASCARPONE ICE CREAM
Whip the cream using a hand mixer.

Place the egg yolks in a bowl. Pour the water and sugar into a saucepan and bring to a boil. When this syrup has reached 244°F (118°C), pour it over the eggs yolks while whisking with an electric mixer on low speed. When all the syrup has been incorporated, beat at high speed until the mixture has cooled.

Stir in the mascarpone, then fold in the whipped cream. Churn the mixture in an ice cream maker or place it in a container in the freezer and stir every hour.

FOR THE STRAWBERRY JELLY
Place the strawberries and sugar in a freezer bag. Seal tightly, removing all the air, then immerse the bag for 30 minutes in a pan of boiling water. Strain through a fine-mesh sieve, without squeezing the contents of the bag, to collect the juice. Soak the gelatin in a bowl of cold water, squeeze it out, then stir into the juice. Pour the jelly into the half-sphere molds. Place in the refrigerator for at least 1 ½ hours. Reserve the rest of the jelly for decoration.

TO SERVE
Mix the red berries with the mustard and the reduced balsamic vinegar. Gently unmold the meringue half spheres and fill half of them with a thin layer of mustard-marinated red berries, then some mascarpone ice cream. Gently place the other meringue half spheres on top to make balls. Place a meringue ball on each plate, then decorate with jelly, seasonal red berries and some dollops of ice cream.

Chef's note

Here, I give pride of place to blackcurrants—Burgundy produce from my adoptive region! The acidity of the blackcurrants and the spiciness of the mustard offset the sweetness of the meringue and the ice cream.

YUZU MUSTARD
SOUFFLÉ

SERVES 4

FOR THE YUZU PASTRY CREAM

3 egg yolks

¼ cup (2 ¼ oz./60 g) superfine sugar

2 tsp. all-purpose flour

1 tbsp. cornstarch

1 cup (250 ml) whole milk

¼ cup (60 ml) yuzu juice

2 ½ tbsp. (1 ½ oz./40 g) yuzu mustard

1 oz. (30 g) mustard bran

FOR THE SOUFFLÉ

1 tbsp. butter, melted

2 ½ tbsp. (1 oz./30 g) superfine sugar, plus 5 tsp. (¾ oz./20 g) for the molds

6 ½ oz. (180 g) egg whites at room temperature (about 6 medium egg whites)

TO FINISH

1 untreated yuzu

FOR THE YUZU PASTRY CREAM

In a bowl, whisk the egg yolks with the sugar, flour, and cornstarch until the mixture turns white. In a saucepan, heat the milk, then add the whisked egg and sugar mixture. Whisk until boiling. Add the yuzu juice, mustard, and mustard bran. Set aside.

FOR THE SOUFFLÉ

Preheat the oven to 360°F (180°C). Brush the insides of four small high-sided porcelain molds with the melted butter, then sprinkle with the 5 teaspoons of sugar.

In a mixing bowl, whisk the egg whites until stiff. Add the sugar and continue whisking, being careful not to over-whisk. Gently fold the egg whites into 7 oz. (200 g) of the yuzu pastry cream. Fill the molds and bake for 12 minutes.

TO FINISH

Remove the soufflés from the oven, sprinkle with finely grated yuzu zest, and serve immediately.

Chef's note

I like to serve light desserts such as this at the end of a meal, to finish on a delicate note. The yuzu, stands out in this recipe and combines with the mustard to sharpen the subtle taste of this dessert.

KEISHI SUGIMURA
LE BÉNATON
BEAUNE

BURGUNDY SNAIL CROQUETTES
WITH TARRAGON DIJON MUSTARD FOAM

MAKES 8

FOR THE CROQUETTES
4 mushrooms, diced
1 oz. (30 g) Morteau sausage, diced
4 tsp. (¾ oz./20 g) butter
32 snails removed from shells
1 oz. (30 g) cooked calf's foot, diced
Leaves from 3 tarragon sprigs, chopped
1 ½ tbsp. tarragon Dijon mustard
Salt and freshly ground pepper

FOR THE BREADCRUMB COATING
Flour
2 eggs, beaten
Breadcrumbs
Vegetable oil for deep-frying

FOR THE TARRAGON MUSTARD FOAM
½ cup (120 ml) whipping cream
Leaves from 2 bunches of tarragon
2 g agar-agar
1 ½ tbsp. tarragon Dijon mustard

TO FINISH
A few mustard greens

FOR THE CROQUETTES
In a pan, sauté the mushrooms and sausage in the butter. Add the snails and the calf's foot. Remove from the heat, then stir in the tarragon and mustard and season with salt and pepper.
Half fill 16 1 ½ inches diameter semi-circular molds with this mixture. Chill for 1 hour, then assemble the semi-circles in pairs to form spheres.

FOR THE BREADCRUMB COATING
Place the flour, beaten eggs, and breadcrumbs on three separate plates, then dip the croquette balls into each in turn.
Pour the vegetable oil into a deep-fat fryer and heat to 340°F (170°C). Gently lower the balls into the oil and cook for 2 to 3 minutes, turning them regularly until they are golden all over. Remove the croquettes from the oil using a slotted spoon, transfer to paper towels, and keep them warm.

FOR THE TARRAGON MUSTARD FOAM
In a saucepan, heat the cream, then add the tarragon leaves. Strain the tarragon cream through a fine-mesh sieve several times, then pour it back into the pan and add the agar-agar and mustard. Bring the cream to a boil, strain again, then pour it into a siphon.

TO FINISH
To serve, place a croquette on each plate, garnish with a few mustard greens and add a little mustard foam using the siphon.

Chef's note
The aromatic freshness of tarragon goes very well with snails. In addition to the harmony of flavors, I like to play on the contrast between the intensity of the mustard and the delicacy of the Burgundy snails.

EGGPLANT WITH BUCKWHEAT

AND DIJON MUSTARD

SERVES 4

FOR THE VIENNOISE
(prepare 1 hour in advance)
2 ¼ oz. (60 g) crackers
⅔ cup (2 ¼ oz./60 g) buckwheat flakes
⅓ cup + 2 tbsp. (3 ½ oz./100 g) butter at room temperature, diced
Salt

FOR THE EGGPLANT
2 graffiti eggplants
Juice of ½ lemon
Salt

TO FINISH
1 tsp. Dijon mustard

FOR THE VIENNOISE
Make the viennoise at least 1 hour in advance. In a food processor or blender, reduce the crackers to breadcrumbs, then add the buckwheat flakes, butter, and a little salt, and process to mix. Spread the mixture between two sheets of parchment paper to a thickness of 1/16 inch (2 mm) and set aside in the freezer.

FOR THE EGGPLANT
Peel the eggplants, then cut them lengthwise into slices 1 ½ inches (4 cm) thick. Drizzle with the lemon juice and season with salt. Wrap each slice separately in plastic wrap and cook in a *bain-marie* for 20 minutes. Leave to cool, then remove the plastic wrap.

TO FINISH
Cut the frozen viennoise according to the size of the eggplant slices. Place a small dot of mustard on each eggplant slice, then cover with a viennoise. Arrange side by side in a heatproof dish and place under the broiler for 3 minutes until golden and crispy. Serve immediately.

Chef's note
As with other recipes, you can make this without mustard, but you would miss out on these spicy little dots of flavor that make your tongue tingle with each bite! Buckwheat has a floury texture and a roasted flavor, while eggplant has a fleshy feel on the palate. The mustard adds a nice little kick to what might otherwise be a rather bland taste.

MACKEREL WITH CHARRED VERMICELLI
AND SEED STYLE DIJON MUSTARD

SERVES 4

FOR THE CHARRED VERMICELLI

7 oz. (200 g) vermicelli

¼ cup (60 ml) dry white wine

¼ cup (60 ml) water

Extra virgin olive oil

FOR THE MACKEREL

4 mackerel (about 8 ¾ oz./250 g each)

Extra virgin olive oil

TO FINISH

1 tbsp. soy sauce

A pinch of minced garlic

1 tsp. seed style Dijon mustard

1 lemon

3 green onions, green parts only, finely chopped

Extra virgin olive oil

Salt and white pepper

FOR THE CHARRED VERMICELLI

In a saucepan, heat a drizzle of olive oil, add the vermicelli and cook without stirring until browned. Pour in the white wine and water, cover the pan, and bring to a boil. Remove from the heat but leave covered for a few minutes to allow the vermicelli to continue cooking until *al dente*.

FOR THE MACKEREL

Preheat the oven to 360°F (180°C). Prepare the mackerel: clean them, remove the heads, lift the fillets, and remove any small bones. Heat a drizzle of olive oil in a rectangular ovenproof dish, then arrange the mackerel fillets in the oil, skin side up, and bake for 2 to 3 minutes.

TO FINISH

Drain the vermicelli, then season with the soy sauce, garlic, mustard, lemon juice, and a drizzle of olive oil. Season with salt and pepper. Divide the vermicelli between the plates and sprinkle with the chopped green onion. Place two mackerel fillets on top and serve immediately.

Chef's notes

I discovered this odd way to cook vermicelli a long time ago in Catalonia. Charring it like this gives it a slightly caramelized flavor. Mackerel is an oily fish so can be quite rich. The spiciness of the mustard restores the balance perfectly, helped by the sharpness of the lemon. Mustard also brings the whole thing together and adds to the creaminess of the dish.

TRIPE WITH RANCIO-STYLE WINE
AND TARRAGON DIJON MUSTARD

SERVES 4

FOR THE TRIPE
(prepare the day before)
1 lb. 9 oz. (700 g) honeycomb beef tripe
1 tsp. coarse salt
1 bouquet garni
1 onion, peeled and cut into large pieces
2 carrots, peeled and cut into large pieces
1 celery stalk, chopped
15 black peppercorns, crushed

FOR THE RELISH
4 fresh walnuts
⅓ oz. (10 g) fresh ginger
½ untreated orange
Juice of ½ lime
4 tsp. hazelnut oil

FOR THE VINAIGRETTE
Scant 1 cup (200 ml) dry rancio-style wine
Scant ¼ cup (50 ml) hazelnut oil
Salt and white pepper

TO FINISH
1 tsp. tarragon Dijon mustard
1 tarragon sprig

FOR THE TRIPE
The day before, cut the tripe into triangles or diamond shapes, then place into a bowl. Cover with cold water and refrigerate overnight.
The next day, rinse the tripe thoroughly and place in a large saucepan with the coarse salt, bouquet garni, onion, carrots, celery and peppercorns. Cover with water and bring to a boil. Remove the scum that rises to the surface and simmer for 5 hours. Check the doneness by removing a piece of tripe – it should be tender.

FOR THE RELISH
Crack and shell the walnuts. Place them in hot, but not boiling, water for 5 minutes so that you can peel them, then break into small pieces. Peel the ginger, then chop into thin sticks. Peel the orange and slice the peel into thin julienne strips. Blanch the orange peel for 30 seconds, then mix with the nuts and ginger. Season with a few drops of lemon juice and hazelnut oil.

FOR THE VINAIGRETTE
In a saucepan, reduce the wine until you have just 4 teaspoons (20 ml) left. Season with a pinch of salt and a grinding of pepper, then whisk in the hazelnut oil.

TO FINISH
Drain the tripe arrange it on the plates, and add a few dots of mustard. Add some relish on top of the tripe and sprinkle with tarragon leaves. Serve the vinaigrette separately.

Chef's note
Rather than diluting the relish with the vinaigrette, I prefer to alternate each bite with a touch of mustard. That way the taste of the mustard really stands out – the spiciness is sensational! It reminds me of when I was a child and used to spread a layer of mustard between slices of bread and Gruyère cheese.

COASTAL ÎLE D'YEU SOLE ROASTED IN SEAWEED BUTTER

WITH GRILLED BABY LEEKS, SHELLFISH, SAMPHIRE, AND LEEK AND PENJA PEPPER MUSTARD MOUSSELINE

SERVES 4

FOR THE SOLE

1 sole, weighing about 2 ¼ lb. (1 kg)
Scant ½ cup (100 ml) olive oil
4 tsp. (20 g) slightly salted butter
Salt and freshly ground pepper

FOR THE SHELLFISH MARINIÈRE

7 oz. (200 g) cockles
7 oz. (200 g) razor clams
1 shallot
Scant ¼ cup (50 ml) olive oil
2 tsp. (10 g) butter
½ celery stalk
1 thyme sprig
1 parsley stalk
1 scant cup (200 ml) dry white wine

FOR THE VEGETABLES

1 onion
A drizzle of olive oil
2 tsp. (10 g) butter
1 lb. 5 oz. (600 g) large leeks
5 oz. (150 g) potato
1 ⅔ cups (400 ml) whipping cream
1 tbsp. Penja pepper mustard
3 ½ oz. (100 g) samphire
4 baby leeks
Salt and Penja pepper

FOR THE SOLE

Ask your fishmonger to skin the sole. In a pan, fry the sole in the olive oil and butter for 2 minutes on each side. Season with salt and pepper. Transfer the sole to a rack to let the flesh rest.

FOR THE SHELLFISH MARINIÈRE

Wash the cockles and razor clams under cold running water. Peel and finely chop the shallot. In a saucepan, heat the olive oil and butter and sauté the shallot, celery, thyme, and parsley. Add the cockles and razor clams. Pour in the white wine and cook, covered, until the shells have opened. Remove the cockles and razor clams from their shells, trim them, and keep them warm. Strain the shellfish broth, reduce in a saucepan and set aside.

FOR THE VEGETABLES

Make the mousseline sauce. Peel and finely chop the onion. In a saucepan, sweat the onion in the olive oil and butter. Wash and chop the large leeks and the potato. Sauté them in the pan with the onion, then stir in the cream. Cook over low heat for 30 minutes, then season with a grinding of Penja pepper and the mustard. Blend everything to a purée. Set aside this mousseline sauce.

Prepare the samphire. Place the samphire in a pan of boiling salted water for 10 seconds to blanch it, then immerse it in a container of ice-cold water to stop it cooking.

Prepare the baby leeks. Cook the leeks in a large pan of boiling salted water for 10 minutes. Drain them and immediately immerse them in a container of ice-cold water. Remove the outer layer from the leeks and squeeze them gently to remove excess water. Sear them on a grill with a drizzle of olive oil. Cut them into sections and season with salt and pepper.

TO SERVE

1 ⅔ cups (400 ml) fish stock

Scant ½ cup (100 ml) whipping cream

1 tsp. Penja pepper mustard

1 tsp. Bordier seaweed butter

¼ oz. (5 g) mixed dried seaweed

1 dill sprig

TO SERVE

Put the fish stock and the reserved shellfish broth into a saucepan and let it reduce. In a separate pan, reduce the whipping cream. Stir the cream into the stock and keep warm.

Just before serving, gently lift the fillets from the sole. Place a dab of mustard between the two fillets and a small knob of seaweed butter on top of the fillets. Reheat in a low oven for 3 minutes. Place the sole fillets onto plates, along with the grilled leeks, shellfish, and samphire. Pour over the mousseline sauce. Decorate with dried seaweed and dill sprigs and serve immediately.

Chef's note

I really like using mustard in my recipes, so I'm lucky to be in Dijon and to be able to use the very best Burgundy mustard, thanks to Maison Fallot. I love peppers and all the different condiments that lift a dish and bring out the flavors of other ingredients. Here, Penja pepper mustard spices up the leek mousseline, grilled leeks and sole. Its subtle strength enlivens the dish and balances its components, adding a fullness and very pleasing warmth at the finish. You could also use it to finish a hollandaise sauce as an accompaniment to this dish. Its spiciness and bite remind me of my West Indian origins.

LIST OF RECIPES

A FAMILY
STORY

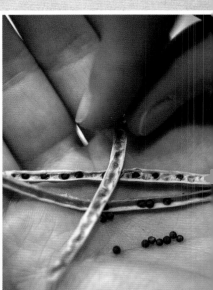

ACKNOWLEDGEMENTS

To have grown up in the heart of this family-owned manufacturing company makes me exceptionally proud. Today it is a great honor for me to head up a company with such a long history of traditional expertise. My encounters with the people who built the history of the Maison Fallot have been particularly inspiring and enriching.

My most heartfelt thanks go to my maternal grandfather, Julien Edmond Fallot, for having so successfully safeguarded our company heritage throughout the testing times of World War II.

Special thanks to my father, Roger Désarménien. In a period of major economic transformation: the advent of the consumer society and the mass distribution, he has managed to preserve the authenticity and the quality within the company.

Thank you to all of our permanent employees – those women and men whose hard work helped to grow our Moutarderie. Also to our customers, who represent our reason for being and the very lifeblood of our enterprise.

Thank you to our suppliers, producers and service-providers whose continued confidence is such a key factor in our sustained growth.

And thank you to our friends, those great chefs who so willingly accepted our invitation to join in this fine project.

Thank you to the team at Éditions de La Martinière, whose professionalism is sure to make this book a vivid testimony to the extraordinary history of the Moutarderie Fallot!

As a natural-born optimist, I know that future generations, starting with Thibault and Yvan, will show themselves more than equal to the challenge of nurturing our enduring success.

Marc Désarménien

Author's acknowledgements

Bénédicte Bortoli wishes to extend her gratitude to the erudite collector Françoise Decloquement for so generously agreeing to share her passion and knowledge; to the entire team at the Moutarderie Fallot for their warm welcome and expert advice on all things mustard; to Marie-Thérèse Garcin for her infectious love of Burgundy; to Jérôme Gervais and Thierry Guinet for their insight into growing practices and Burgundy mustard seeds; and to Marie-Amélie Clercant at Éditions de La Martinière for her confidence throughout the writing of this book.

The editor would like to thank the Chefs, Pastry Chefs and Head Bartenders who agreed to participate in this book.

Photographic Credits
Page 14: ©akg-images; Page 17: ©BnF, Bibliothèque Nationale de France, département Estampes and photography; Page 19: ©Alinari/Bridgeman images; Page 23: ©A.Dagli Orti: De Agostini Picture Library/Bridgeman images; Page 28: DR Private Collection; Pages 33, 34, 35: DR/ Private Collection Moutarderie Fallot; Page 43: ©Images Florilegius/Bridgeman images; Page 72: Scheme by Yvan Désarménien; Pages 186-187, 188 (bottom, left): © La Moutarderie Fallot

Text: Bénédicte Bortoli
Photographs: Matthieu Cellard
Food and cover styling: Laure Maso , Labelaure
The photographed recipes were made by Chef Sébastien Chambru of l'O des Vignes in Fuissé.

Graphic design and Layout: Justeciel
Recipe editing: Carine Merlin
Body text English translation and proofreading: Flo Brutton
Recipe translation: Anne McDowall

Copyright ©2020, Éditions de La Martinière, an imprint of EDLM for the original and English translation
10 9 8 7 6 5 4 3 2 1

Abrams books are available at special discounts when purchased in quantity for premiums and promotions as well as fundraising or educational use. Special editions can also be created to specification.
For details, contact specialsales@abramsbooks.com or the address below.

Photoengraving: Chromostyle
Printed and bound in September 2020 by Pollina (France)
Legal Deposit: october 2020
ISBN: 978-1-4197-5284-1

ABRAMS The Art of Books
195 Broadway, New York, NY 10007
abramsbooks.com